STOP THE HACK *Before* It Happens

LEARN HOW TO FIGHT AGAINST CYBERSECURITY THREATS

Rafeeq Al-Hashemi, Ph.D.

Copyright © 2024

All rights reserved.

Book Description

In today's era of information technology and artificial intelligence, it's imperative to safeguard your assets against cyber-attacks. Cybercriminals seek every possible way to steal personal and financial information. Threats are on the rise everywhere. A data breach could bring financial ruin to an individual or a company. Failure to educate yourself about these threats and the countermeasures to mitigate them is a risk you can no longer afford to take in the current era of high technology.

STOP THE HACK offers a detailed guide that empowers you to recognize the main cyber risks and take the proper preventive measures to defend your digital assets.

This book introduces you to the most common cyber threats and methods that attackers use. It shows you how to identify the most common symptoms and prevent or reduce the effects of such attacks. And it gives you a list of best practices that you can use to protect the sensitive information on your computer, phone, network, and social media profile.

The book starts from the basics and moves to more advanced cybersecurity topics, but prior knowledge of cyber technology is not required for one to benefit from the information herein. I have done my best to write it in a way that everyday people–students, parents, employers, small businesses owners–can grasp. Videos illustrating the step-by-step processes are available to support the text. Please check my YouTube Channel below:

https://www.youtube.com/@DrRafeeq

Book Disclaimer

The information and material in this publication are for general guidance and knowledge, and the author and publisher make no guarantees about their accuracy, reliability, suitability, or availability.

This book is based on the author's research, knowledge, and personal experience. The content does not represent the position of any organization or entity. Moreover, the author is not liable for any losses, damages, or harm as a result of using or misusing the information provided herein. This book is not intended as professional guidance. Every effort has been made to honor copyright and intellectual property rights. All rights reserved. No part of this book can be reproduced without written permission. By reading this book, you acknowledge and agree to the terms and conditions of this disclaimer.

DEDICATION

I dedicate this book to my father, Dr. Al-Hashimi, for shaping me into the person I am today through his guidance and support. His wisdom and patience have been invaluable to me.

I also dedicate this book to my mother, whose unwavering faith and devotion have inspired and strengthened me. Her love has given me the courage to pursue my dreams.

To my wife, your support and encouragement have been invaluable to me. Your belief in my abilities has helped me push past my doubts, and your love and understanding have given me the strength to aim for the stars.

My kids Ayham, Aws, and Reemas, this book is dedicated to you as a testament to my love for you and my commitment to making the world a better place for you. Remember that you can achieve anything you set your mind to. With heartfelt gratitude,

Rafeeq

TABLE OF CONTENTS

Chapter 1: Cyber Security Common Threats 11
   1.1   Types of malicious code 11
      Backdoor 12
      Viruses 13
      VIRUS types 13
      Worms 15
      Trojan horses 15
      Spyware 16
      Rootkit 16
      Logic bomb 17
      Ransomware 18
   1.2   Authentication/Authorization threats 18
   Password Attacks 19
   Social Engineering 21
Phishing 28
Vishing 29
Methods To Acquire and Misuse Personal, Confidential Data to Commit Identity Theft 30
   1.3   How attackers target online shoppers 34
Chapter 2: How to Protect Yourself 36
   2.1   tax identity theft protection 36
   2.2   Prevent Medical Identity Theft 36
   2.3   Take extra precautions to protect yourself 37
   2.4   HOW TO protect yourself online 42
Chapter 3: Chapter 3: Countermeasures 47
   3.1   Password measures 48

3.2	authentication	49
3.3	secure networks	50
3.4	Windows Login Password Policy	52
3.4.1	Enforce Password History	55
3.4.2	Maximum password age	56
3.4.3	Minimum password age	56
3.4.4	Minimum password length	56
3.4.5	Password must meet complexity requirements.	57
3.4.6	Store passwords using reversible encryption.	58
3.5	Account Lockout Policy in Windows	58
3.5.1	Account lockout threshold for Invalid logins	60
3.5.2	Account lockout duration	60
3.5.3	Enabling two-step authentication on Facebook	61
3.6	Recommended countermeasures on your smartphone	66
3.7	How to resist malware	71
3.8	Ransomware System-Level Protection	73
3.9	ransomware Network-Level Protection	75
3.10	Measures In the event of a Ransomware Attack	76
3.11	Wrapping Up and Looking Ahead	77
3.12	Security Tip	78
3.12.1	Evaluating Your Web Browser's Security Settings	78
3.12.2	The significance of security settings for web browsers	78
3.12.3	Where can you find the settings?	79
3.12.4	How do you know what your settings should be	80
3.12.5	What do the different terms mean	80
3.13	How to minimize the risks to your wireless net	83
3.14	How To Enable Two-Factor Authentication On Gmail And Google.	86
3.15	tips that can help avoid a spyware attack	95

- 3.16 How to Detect Spyware 97
  - Homepage HIJACKING 98
  - Redirected web searches 98
  - Performance problems 98
  - Inundation of Pop-up ads 99
  - Expensive phone bills 99
  - Overly active modem activity 99
  - Files mysteriously change 99
  - 3.16.1 CD tray with a mind of its own 99
  - Unidentified sent emails 100
- 3.17 Trojan Horse Prevention 100
- 3.18 How do you recognize a sniffer? 100
  - 3.18.1 SNIFFEER REMOVAL PROCEDURE 101
  - 3.18.2 HOW TO PREVENT SNIFFER 101
  - 3.18.3 HOW TO PROTECT YOURSELF FROM A SNIFFER 102
- 3.19 Artificial Intelligence and Cybersecurity: 102
  - 3.19.1 Advanced Malware Detection 103
- 3.20 AI Cybersecurity Countermeasures 103
- 3.21 Top 7 Cyber Security Tools That Use AI 104

Chapter 4: Best practices 105
- 3.22 Operating System: 105
- 3.23 Internet/Networks 111
- 3.24 Social media 113
- 3.25 Mobile Safety Tips 113
- 3.26 Holiday Traveling with Personal Internet-Enabled Devices 114
- 3.27 Important resources 116
7. References 119

Introduction

In the information age that we live in, cyber threats are on the rise everywhere. Hackers and attackers have numerous ways to infiltrate your computers and gain access to your personal and financial information. If you don't educate yourself about these dangers, and take countermeasures to mitigate them, you risk losing everything that is of value to you.

Consider:

In March 2017, Equifax, a credit reporting agency in the US, fell victim to one of the biggest data breaches in history. Hackers obtained the personal information of 143 million Equifax customers. The breached information included social security numbers, driver's license numbers, dates of birth, addresses, and more.

In May 2023 T-Mobile, the second-largest wireless carrier in America, suffered its second major data breach of the year and its *ninth* since 2018. In one that occurred in November 2022, personal information from over 37 million customers was lifted.

Even cybersecurity companies are not immune to hacks. In January 2023, Norton LifeLock, a major cybersecurity provider, had sensitive information of over 6,000 customers stolen by cybercriminals.

These kinds of mass breaches occur all the time all over the world. It happens to corporations that should know better and be better prepared–especially cyber security companies!

Nor are just corporate entities vulnerable. Individuals and families are also the target of cyber thieves. *STOP THE HACK* is an introduction to cyber security. Its objective is to provide you with the knowledge you need to safeguard yourself against cyberattacks.

To that end, this book:

- lays out the most common threats and attacker tactics.

- offers guidance in recognizing the symptoms of such threats and in understanding their potential consequences.

- offers specific preventative measures you can take to protect your system, computer, phone, network, and social media profile.

All it takes to lose everything is one weak password, one reflexive click on an unknown attachment, one mindless reply to an ensnaring email. You lock your car doors. You secure and monitor your house. Why would you not take the same level of precaution with your other valuable assets–your finances, your savings, your personal information, your social profile? All that is precious to you can be wiped away in an instant, with a single stroke of a key.

A caveat: It's important to understand that there's no one specific measure you can take to protect your information. Protection requires many things, including personal awareness, employing effective countermeasures, implementing the right policies, applying physical measures, following good practices, and more. There's no single magical step you can take to be completely protected.

Chapter 1: CYBER SECURITY COMMON THREATS

This chapter covers the most common IT threats and their behaviors. A threat/attack can take many shapes and forms. Here are some of them:

1- Malware attack

2- Authentication/Authorization

3- Social engineering attack

4- System vulnerabilities

1.1 TYPES OF MALICIOUS CODE

Malware, also known as malicious code, is software that is designed to cause harm. Attackers create malware to gain unauthorized access to your private or sensitive information, or to monitor your activities. As a computer user, you need to understand the various threats that malware poses, and to familiarize yourself with the measures you can take to best defend against those threats. The most vulnerable targets are computer users who are unaware of the security risks. Lack of knowledge and failure to take protective measures make it easier for attackers to carry out their malicious actions.

Attackers vary their code and installation methods depending on their objectives. For instance, malware can delete files or create a gateway for unauthorized users to infiltrate a system. Being cognizant of the different types of threats makes you less susceptible to attack. In the forthcoming chapter, we will introduce you to the various types of malware. We will explain their behaviors and show you how to detect them.

Here are some common forms of malware:

- Backdoor
- Viruses
- Worms
- Trojan horses
- Spyware
- Rootkit
- Logic bomb
- Ransomware

Let's look at each of these, one by one.

BACKDOOR

As the name implies, a backdoor is a way to gain unauthorized access to a system. It accomplishes this by bypassing the standard authentication mechanism. The backdoor access method is written by malware developers to obtain unrestricted access to the system in the future.

Viruses

A virus is a malicious code. The main difference between a virus and other malware is that the virus works by cloning and attaching itself to an executable file, such as files with the extension (.exe).

A virus is activated when the executable code runs, at which point it reproduces itself in order to infect additional files.

Virus types

Boot Sector Virus – Is a type of a virus that infects the most critical part of the hard disk drive (HDD), the boot sector portion. When a computer is turned on, it starts "booting," which means it launches the operating system (OS) from the boot sector of the HDD. After booting, it loads the other required files from different portions of the HDD.

This malware infects the booting sector of the HDD by releasing its virus before the Antivirus software is loaded. Pre-empting the Antivirus software makes the virus hard to detect and remove.

Program Virus – This type of virus attaches itself to executable files. It's programmed to execute the virus before the original program runs, making it very difficult to detect. One of the methods used to defend against a program virus is a program called Checksum. Checksum compares the current file size to the original file size– before opening the file. If any changes have been made, it's likely that something has been added, such as, possibly, a malicious code. Thus Checksum detects the virus before it damages a system.

Macro Virus – This type of virus works by embedding harmful code in the macros of the documents. Most Macro viruses are transmitted through email attachments. Therefore, caution must always be exercised before opening any attachment, such as a word document, as it might contain malicious code. This type of virus is very common, and you need to be alert to it. Never click on an email link or open an attached document if you don't recognize the sender or are not expecting an attachment from the sender. When in doubt, the best practice is to verify first: Contact the sender to ensure that they in fact sent you the attachment, especially if it seems suspicious.

STEALTH VIRUS

This kind of virus attempts to hide from the Antivirus software. To avoid detection, it can conceal the size of the infected file. For example, in active mode, it hides its modifications in files or boot records.

Polymorphic Virus – This virus is similar to the stealth virus, as it also hides to avoid detection. But the polymorphic virus is different because it changes itself, making its code difficult to identify. Every virus has its own signature. Antiviruses scan files looking for one of those signatures. The polymorphic virus, however, changes its signature occasionally to avoid such detection.

The following chapters will show you how to defend against Malware threats using best practices.

WORMS

Worms are different from viruses. Viruses attach themselves to files, while Worms are standalone files that can be distributed throughout the network. A virus is system-based Malware; a Worm is network-based. Worms can spread through an attachment or a link in an email.

TROJAN HORSES

In contrast to a virus, a Trojan horse is standalone malware. It is hidden in the software, and attaches itself to other files. To make it work, the attacker must trick the user into installing and running the program that it's embedded in. The hidden functions will execute only after the Trojan horse is installed.

Trojan horses spy on your computer and steal your sensitive information. They can also generate backdoor access to your system or remote access to your computer. This kind of malware can do many harmful things, including deleting files, modifying data, copying data, among other criminal acts.

Spyware

Spyware is a type of malware that is infiltrated into a user's system without their knowledge and gathers the victim's personal data, such as passwords or credit card numbers. Spyware can also record and send to the attacker every keystroke the user makes. It basically keeps track of everything a user does while online, whether surfing, shopping, or any other activity.

A user can become a victim of spyware when accessing a compromised website or opening an infected email, etc.

Rootkit

Among all the types of Malware, rootkit is the most dangerous. It's built to alter and modify the operating system. This kind of malware can take control of your operating system. For instance, it can give privileged access to your computer, log every keystroke you hit on the keyboard, and create a backdoor.

Rootkit is hard to detect for many reasons. First, it's loaded before the operating system is turned on. Second, it may corrupt the Antivirus. And third, it hides itself, and can even spread by itself.

Rootkit can be inadvertently installed by various means, including email phishing, sharing an infected drive, downloading and executing a malicious file, among other ways.

One sign that you are infected by Rootkit is that your Antivirus doesn't work. Another sign is that you experience an unplanned or unexplained change in your system's settings.

LOGIC BOMB

Logic bombs are malicious codes that an authorized user installs. They are especially hard to detect, as the malicious code is triggered by a future event. One of the best ways to mitigate the damage from a logic bomb is simply to back up your system.

The huge mortgage enterprise Fannie Mae terminated the contract of a programmer in 2008. The programmer was able to implant a logic bomb before his access to the network was cut off. The logic bomb was intended to attack and destroy all the data of the company. Fortunately, it was detected before it executed its payload. The programmer received a sentence of 41 months in prison.

A time bomb is a form of logic bomb malware. Time bombs release their malicious payload at a specified time. (Conklin, 2016)

RANSOMWARE

Ransomware is sometimes called a "drive-by download," which means it is enabled by the victim's unintentional download of the malicious code from the internet. Ransomware attackers trick the user into downloading and installing the ransomware onto his or her computer. CryptoLocker is one example of Ransomware. It is triggered after installation, and ciphers all the victim's data on the infected computer. The attacker then demands a sum of money (ransom payment) to decipher the encrypted information.

1.2 AUTHENTICATION/AUTHORIZATION THREATS

To access any system, a user must complete two steps: Authentication and Authorization. Authentication verifies who the user is. The most common authentication mechanism is username and password. Authentication is the first step. The second step is determining what permissions you have. This process is known as Authorization.

There are many kinds of attacks against the Authentication/ Authorization process. These are some of the most frequent:

- Password attack
- Birthday attack
- Social Engineering
- Pharming
- Phishing/ Vishing

Let's look at each one.

PASSWORD ATTACKS

We usually use a combination of username and password to identify a user. For that reason, the password is a common target for the attacker. There are several methods to steal passwords, including:

Guessing – Choosing a weak password makes the hacker's job easier. Many users employ a well-known or common word, or use the default password or a password related to personal information, such as the user's name, date of birth, and car name. Some people, of course, use "password" as their password.

In the coming chapters, you will be introduced to the best methods for choosing a strong password.

Dictionary attack - Sometimes an attacker uses a password dictionary to ascertain a password. This dictionary has a list of common passwords as well as everyday English words. Such software has the ability to test virtually all of the possible standard passwords. However, it is not successful against passwords with combinations of characters such as capital and small letters, or numbers and symbols.

Brute-force attack – If the user is conscientious enough to select a password that's not in the dictionary, the attacker can try an alternative invasive method called a Brute-force attack. A Brute-force method runs through all possible combinations of letters, symbols, and numbers. It's very time-consuming, but is now feasible with today's faster, more powerful computers. It's important to note that the length of the password is a significant parameter in impeding this process.

A hybrid attack combines both dictionary and brute-force methodology. The hybrid is a common approach used in many password-cracking tool boxes. The dictionary attack is tried first, followed by brute-force methods. Attackers employ programs that generate word-combination passwords, such as when users replace letters with numbers, for example utilizing "s3cr3t" instead of the word "secret" to create a password that is both strong and easy to remember. While "s3cr3t" may not be found in a dictionary attack, it could be uncovered easily by an attacker who combines a dictionary attack with a brute-force attack.

BIRTHDAY ATTACK - This method gets its name from a theory known as the birthday paradox. It is a specific kind of brute-force attack. The birthday paradox states that in a random sampling of only 23 people there is a better than 50% chance that two individuals within the group of 23 will share the same birthday. (It's true and is based on a sophisticated mathematical equation.) This phenomenon applies to passwords, too, although it requires a somewhat larger sampling.

SOCIAL ENGINEERING

Social engineering is a general term covering a wide range of illicit activities that focus on human interaction rather than on technology. Such an attack involves gaining access to confidential information by using some form of deceit or misrepresentation to manipulate authorized users into revealing confidential information. The following are types of social engineering attacks.

SNIFFING is an attack that captures and monitors the data passing through a network. Sniffing malware acquires the contents of packets and searches for sensitive information, such as passwords, accounts, or anything of value. There are many tools available on the internet that attackers can use to capture network traffic–tools such as Wireshark, EtherPeek, and others. These applications were created for legitimate purposes, mainly to collect and analyze information in order to debug and troubleshoot problems. However, attackers have found a way to utilize them for their own malicious purposes.

SPOOFING is an attack in which illegitimate users employ a false identity to gain entrance into a targeted system. Spoofing uses a fake identity to gain access to specified email or IP addresses. Once in, an attacker can collect sensitive information, delete data, or even damage the system.

MAN-IN-THE-MIDDLE (MITM) attack is similar to the sniffing attack but employs more sophisticated processes that allow the attacker to implement various kinds of attacks. MITM is an active attack, whereas sniffing is a passive one. The attacker in the MITM sniffs, monitors, and alters data. He or she steals a user's identity and changes the messages between the two sites on both ends of the communication.

KEYLOGGER enables an attacker to surreptitiously monitor a user's activity, either by way of a small hardware device or a malware code. The hardware device, which can be connected to the keyboard or placed between the keyboard and the computer, captures every keystroke. This type of attack can collect sensitive information, such as passwords, chat history, and screenshots of the user's activities, etc.

VULNERABILITIES are weaknesses either in the system or the software that allow attackers to gain unauthorized access to sensitive information.

BUFFER OVERFLOW can occur when the developer/programmer does not validate or set some constraints on the user input. If the user intentionally or unintentionally enters a number longer than the scope of the storage limit of that field of data, it can cause an overflow. For example, if the first name field is limited to no more than 20 characters, and the user enters, say, twenty-five characters, the input will be detected and rejected by the system. The absence of input validation can give the attacker the opportunity to utilize this vulnerability to damage the system or overwrite or corrupt other data stored in its memory.

DENIAL-OF-SERVICE (DOS) prevents legitimate users from accessing their systems. It can also slow down the system, or block system functions, or make the system/network/servers inaccessible. DOS attackers employ different methods. He or she can use a system's or network's protocol vulnerabilities to flood the server or otherwise disturb the network, causing it to crash. In the process, the system or network runs slower than normal, and certain websites may become inaccessible.

A DRIVE-BY DOWNLOAD ATTACK can be achieved by downloading and installing malware on a victim's computer without the victim's knowledge. The attackers may insert a malicious code into, or otherwise alter, a legitimate website. When the victim opens the hacked site, the malicious code is automatically downloaded and installed onto the victim's computer without his or her knowledge.

AN INJECTION ATTACK inputs code into a program or a website, in order to modify the program's or website's data. It can also be used to change or retrieve data from a database. There are many different types of injection attacks. One is called SQL Injection (structured query language). Here, the attacker inserts an SQL statement in order to allow him/her to retrieve information that is normally accessible to authorized users only. This is made possible when a system or website has vulnerabilities, such as when the user inserts SQL statements in the field of username, tricking the system into allowing the attacker in or retrieving information from the database. So it's imperative to patch any vulnerabilities and keep the applications up to date.

PIGGYBACKING is the practice of illegally gaining access to another person's system by using their authorization. An unsecure or weak wireless network is vulnerable to piggybacking. Any wireless-enabled device within range of an access point can be exploited. The broadcast range of a typical indoor access point is 150 to 300 feet, and of a typical outdoor access point is 1,000 feet. If your neighborhood is densely populated, or if you live in an apartment complex, for example, you are vulnerable to the interception and monitoring of your online activity.

WARDRIVING is a form of piggybacking in which the bad actors drive around neighborhoods using a Wi-Fi-equipped laptop with a strong antenna, searching for unsecured wireless networks. Wardriving is made possible by the wide coverage area of Wi-Fi access points, which often enables internet connectivity beyond the building's walls, sometimes as far as the street.

EVIL TWIN ATTACKS occur when a cybercriminal acquires the details of a public network access point and uses his/her system to create a twin (a faked copy) of the actual access point. He then transmits a stronger signal than the original router/access point, duping an unwitting victim into connecting into his/her system. Attackers use hacking tools to intercept any data transmitted by the victim over the internet, including credit card numbers, usernames, passwords, and other personal information. Therefore, it's crucial to verify the name and password of the public Wi-Fi hotspot. This will ensure that you are connected to secure Wi-Fi.

WIRELESS SNIFFING: Public Wi-fi may lack encryption or other security measures. Such open, unrestricted connections are susceptible to malicious actors who may utilize sniffing tools to intercept confidential information. Therefore, it's crucial to verify that the Wi-Fi utilizes, at a minimum, WPA2 encryption.

UNAUTHORIZED COMPUTER ACCESS: Unsecured file-folder sharing is risky, especially on an unsecured public wireless network. Any files or directories that you share on a public network are potentially at risk, so the best practice in this case is to disable your file sharing. If you must share, do so only on a recognized network. And don't forget to turn off the sharing mode as soon as you're finished.

SHOULDER SURFING: Perhaps the simplest way to steal confidential information is for an attacker to surreptitiously read off your personal device while you're using it. The best way to prevent this is by acquiring a screen protector. Protectors are inexpensive and effective and easy to use. Also, it's always a good practice to be aware of one's surroundings when entering a password or reading through confidential information.

THEFT OF MOBILE DEVICES: Of course, attackers don't necessarily need to use wireless methods to access your data. They can simply steal your device, giving them unrestricted access to all your data, including connected cloud accounts.

Of course, everyone should take precautions to safeguard their devices against theft or loss. However, if such an unfortunate event happens, you can still take precautionary steps in advance to prevent the loss of valuable data. Most mobile devices, including laptops, allow you to encrypt your stored data. This renders the device unusable to attackers unless they can provide the correct password or PIN.

In addition to encrypting the contents of your device, you can also configure your device's applications to prompt login credentials before accessing any cloud-based information.

IDENTITY THEFT: This is a general term for the act of stealing someone's sensitive information, such as their name or SSN, with the intention of engaging in fraudulent activity. Cybercriminals can use your identity to apply for a credit card, for example, or file tax returns illegally. It's possible that you may not even realize you've been targeted until you start experiencing financial issues. You might receive unexpected bills, debt collections, or loan rejections, all resulting from the thief's use of your stolen identity. Among other things, these actions can severely damage your credit standing. Recovering from such theft takes a lot of time, effort, and money.

There are several other kinds of identity theft: child ID theft, medical insurance theft, tax ID theft, senior ID theft, and SSN theft. Child ID theft can be especially challenging, as it can go undetected for years and ultimately affect the child's identity when he or she reaches adulthood. Tax ID theft occurs when a cybercriminal uses someone's

SSN to file fraudulent taxes (in order to receive an expected refund). Medical ID theft occurs when a thief steals personal health-related information, such as Medicare or health insurance member numbers, and uses it to obtain medical services or submit false claims to the health insurance providers. Senior ID thieves, as the name suggests, target older adults. The elderly may be more susceptible to fraud because of their frequent medical appointments. They are also vulnerable by way of their health providers, who have sensitive personal or financial information that can be tapped into by cyber thieves. Finally, Social ID theft occurs when a malicious actor uses a person's identity (name or picture or personal information) to create a fake social media account.

PHISHING

Phishing, which involves identity and credential theft, is one of the most common types of cyberattack. Phishers often send normal-looking emails or instant messages, pretending to be a legitimate business enterprise seeking to help you. Their email might include a link to a website that appears to be Amazon, eBay, PayPal, or a bank, etc., asking you to log in. However, after clicking on their link, you are surreptitiously directed to a fake website, where you are asked for confidential information, such as your password, credit card number, or bank account number. This kind of attack is called "pharming." A similar technique attackers use is to send you an email informing you that your bank account has been compromised and requesting you to verify your identity by entering your username and password into the attached link.

Ultimately, the best defense against phishing attacks is awareness and education. Regular training of users and employees—including learning about newly developing trends—is critical. This book thoroughly covers the most common types of cyberattacks and newly emerging cyberthreats. It is an invaluable resource for you, your family, friends, students, and employees to help you defend against the highly risky dark world of cybercrime.

VISHING

Vishing is a phishing attack that uses voice instead of emails or texts. People sometimes trust phone calls more than emails. Vishing attackers are able to spoof calls by using Voice Over IP (VOIP). VOIP allows an attacker to use a phone number from the same area code as the victim. Once you pick up your phone, the attacker might use subtle ways to induce you to reveal your sensitive information. For example, he/she may pretend to be an employee of your bank and ask you to confirm your account information. Or he/she might pose as a government employee and inform you that you risk losing your health insurance or your monthly Social Security checks. This kind of crafty coercion can be enough to impel some people to share their confidential information with a stranger.

One potential warning signal of a vishing attack is an unsolicited call in which the caller urgently needs some basic or publicly available information, such as your home address. Once you respond, he might follow up with a more confidential request, such as your password or your bank account number.

Methods To Acquire and Misuse Personal, Confidential Data to Commit Identity Theft

Individuals who steal identities do so in various ways, including:

- Dumpster diving, which means searching through garbage to obtain private information. In some cases, a thief can recover a USB drive or even discarded electronic devices, such as computers, smart phones, or servers, which he can mine for personal information. Such devices might have been carelessly thrown away, given away, or sold without ensuring proper data erasure.

- Obtaining an individual citizen's public records, which are typically available in official databases, such as electoral registers.

- Obtaining credit cards, IDs, passports, and tokens used for authentication, which are often stolen from mailboxes or during house break-ins.

- Obtaining confidential account information by answering common questions, such as "What's your mother's maiden name?", "What model was your first car?", or "What was the name of your first pet?" Acquiring such information could occur when unsuspecting people are asked to fill out a fake questionnaire or apply for approval to gain access to a bogus business or account.

- Illegally gathering data from banks or credit cards by making a duplicate card using a hacked or portable card reader.

- Acquiring data from RFID-enabled devices by using wireless credit card readers that are 'contactless.' RFID stands for "radio-frequency identification." RFID uses a microchip that contains sensitive information, such as your full name, address, and biometrics. It is used in some employee IDs, security access cards, highway toll tags, and passports, among many other things. RFID information is vulnerable because it can be accessed without making physical contact, simply by swiping at it from a distance. (Note: Passports can be accessed only when the front cover is opened.)

- Surreptitiously watching or listening to others as they provide personal information (known as "shoulder-surfing"), which is commonly done in crowded areas where it's relatively easy to observe someone entering their ATM PINs or passwords on their smart devices.

- Gaining access to an individual's personal data by exploiting browser security vulnerabilities, or utilizing malevolent software, such as keystroke loggers, a Trojan horse, or Spyware.

- Stealing personal data by hacking a computer network or a database.

- Taking advantage of security breaches that allow an attacker access to personal details, such as Social Security numbers and credit card numbers, etc.

- Posting fake job openings or other opportunities to acquire CVs and job applications that reveal the candidates' personal data, such as their name, addresses, phone numbers, email addresses, and occasionally banking information.

- Abusing the privileged access of IT users who have insider knowledge of how to retrieve personal information from the employers' databases.

- Penetrating the records of enterprises that contain or handle valuable or confidential individual data, or sometimes even gaining access to substantial quantities of individual data.

- Pretending via email, SMS texts, calls, or other means of communication to be a reputable entity with the intention of tricking victims into revealing their credentials or personal information. This is known as phishing and is typically achieved through a counterfeit business webpage, or data collection forms.

- Using brute force attacks on weak passwords or employing educated guesswork on weak password reset questions.

- Acquiring fingerprint impressions to fabricate false fingerprints for the purpose of identification.

- Searching social media platforms to obtain personal information shared by users, then utilizing that information to enhance credibility during subsequent social engineering endeavors.

- Redirecting victims' emails or mail to obtain sensitive data, such as credit card information, billing statements, and bank/credit card statements. This tactic could also delay the detection of fraudulently opened accounts and credit agreements in the victim's name.

- Deceiving help-desk employees into revealing personal information or modifying user passwords or user access rights through false pretenses. This tactic is known as "pretexting."

- Acquiring banking information, such as account numbers and bank codes, by stealing checks.

- Using information obtained from social networks such as Facebook and Myspace to make educated guesses about Social Security numbers.

- Downloading photos on social networking sites and using them for malicious intent. (Photos can be easily clicked and downloaded).

- Befriending an unsuspecting victim on a social network and exploiting their trust to obtain private information.

1.3 HOW ATTACKERS TARGET ONLINE SHOPPERS

Attackers take advantage of online shoppers in three common ways. First, by creating fraudulent websites or email messages that appear legitimate but are used to deceive shoppers into giving up personal or sensitive information. Second, by intercepting unsecured transactions, which can occur when a vendor fails to employ encryption during the transmission process. Third, by targeting vulnerable computers, particularly by gaining access to a shopper's computer that is unprotected and therefore vulnerable to viruses or other malicious code. It's important to note that vendors also have a responsibility to protect their computers and their customer databases to prevent attackers from gaining access.

Chapter 2: How to Protect Yourself

2.1 TAX IDENTITY THEFT PROTECTION

Filing your income taxes early helps to protect yourself from tax identity theft. An early filing makes it more difficult for a thief to successfully file taxes using your identity. You should also be on the lookout for any IRS letters or notices indicating one of the following: that several tax returns were filed with your SSN; that additional taxes are owed; that tax refunds were offset; or that collection actions were initiated for a year in which you did not file a tax return (even though you actually filed that year). Such notifications could mean that you are a victim of identity theft. Receiving wages from an unknown employer is also a potential indicator of identity theft.

It's always a good practice to ignore suspicious links in text messages, emails, or messages in social media. Also, it's advisable to notify the IRS if you notice any suspicious activities.

2.2 PREVENT MEDICAL IDENTITY THEFT

To prevent medical identity theft, it's essential to take specific defensive measures. Protect your SSN, Medicare, and health insurance ID numbers. Make sure to give these numbers only to authorized healthcare providers, such as your physician. Also, carefully examine your explanation of benefits or your Medicare

Summary Notice, in order to confirm that the billed services align with the services you received. If you detect any suspicious charges, report them immediately to your health insurance provider. Finally, it's important to request a duplicate of your medical records and meticulously review them for any inaccuracies or conditions that do not apply to you.

2.3 TAKE EXTRA PRECAUTIONS TO PROTECT YOURSELF

- Do your homework before buying any product and do business only with reputable vendors – Do not provide your personal information or your credentials to unverified websites or vendors. Do business only with well-known vendors. Attackers may spoof a vendor's IP address, mimic the original website, and trick the user into entering his or her credentials into the illegitimate website. Double-check the link, and make sure it's spelled correctly. Sometimes bogus websites have just one letter different from the original one. For example, if you look carefully at www.amaz0n.com, you can see that the letter 'o' is replaced with '0' in this URL.

- Ensure your information is encrypted – Do not enter your credentials or sensitive information into unsecured websites. Ensure that the website you are trying to use is secure by checking the lock icon on the address bar. If the icon isn't showing on the address (URL), avoid the website. Also, be sure it uses a secure sockets layer or HTTPS: protocol.

Do not enter your credentials in an unencrypted site, even one that uses (HTTP :) protocol. If a site is unencrypted, it means the traffic and the data you enter will be sent as plain, unencrypted text, and anyone who intercepts the connection can read your data as clear text.

- Be wary of emails requesting information – Be suspicious of every email whose source you do not know. Be particularly wary of any incoming email that asks you to confirm your purchase, or to enter your credentials in order to confirm the transaction.

 Do not click on such a link immediately. Instead, you can type it by yourself on the browser or go directly to the original website and log in, in order to double-check and track your transactions. A legitimate business does not request your credentials by email. Just go to the business's website or call them to verify that the email came from a legitimate source.

- Never use a debit card to pay for online transactions – Always use a low-limit credit card to shop online. Credit cards are safer and have limits. Connect your Apple Pay, or PayPal account to one limited credit card, in order to minimize any potential damage, just in case.

- Check your shopping app settings – Do your homework and double-check the app's security and privacy settings. Default settings are not optimal for security. You'll need to change your security and privacy setting to something that is optimal for you and your policy. You can determine how secure to make your settings by finding out how the app handles your data, information, and privacy..

- Check your statements – Review your receipts and keep copies of the statements for your record. Double-check and compare these copies to your bank statement at the end of each month. Immediately report any transactions that are inaccurate or that you don't recognize.

- Engage with your children on the computer. Play games with them, do research with them, teach them positive habits. Explain to them the dangers of online activity, and how to identify suspicious behavior.

- Check privacy policies – Carefully review the privacy policy of each website and app you are accessing before providing any personal information. Find out where your data will be stored and how your information will be handled. If it's handled by a third party, your risk is increased.

- Be involved - Engage with your children. Keep track of their activities and monitor their online behavior. Show your kids how to identify suspicious activity and warn them about the risk associated with sharing private information online. Advise them to share their information only with individuals they know and trust. Let your kids be aware of cyber risks, but do so without instilling fear. Also, discuss the issue of cyberbullying and how to handle it. (For further helpful information on this topic, review the resource "Dealing with Cyberbullies.")

- Computer location- Keep your computer in a visible place, so you can monitor your kids' activities, and take immediate action to control the computer in case you see any inappropriate or harmful behavior. Set guidelines and rules, such as setting a time limit on usage, and determining which websites, apps, and activities are permitted. We recommend determining which sites and apps they can and cannot have access to. Show your kids which computer activity is acceptable and safe and which ones are not. Your child must understand the boundaries of acceptable computer activity. The guidelines must be appropriate for their age, and skill level. It is crucial to monitor your children's computer activity. For their own safety and the security of your online information, we recommend that you find out which websites they visit and who they communicate with through social media, email, or instant messaging.

- We highly recommend that you partition your computer into multiple user accounts. By creating a separate account for your child, you minimize the risk of your kids unintentionally accessing, modifying, or deleting your files. You can achieve this by reducing their level of access and their privileges. Creating separate user accounts for each individual user through the operating system adds a strong level of security to your overall system.

If you don't have separate accounts, then extra caution must be taken with regard to security settings. In addition to restricting functionality through the browser, it's also best to avoid storing password and personal information by your browser. We also recommend keeping a list of the latest virus names and descriptions.

- One option you can consider is to use parental controls. For instance, Internet Explorer offers the ability to limit or permit access to specific websites on your device, with the option of safeguarding these configurations by using a password. In order to access these features, click the Tools option in the menu, select the "Internet Options", select the "Content tab", and then select the Enable (...) button under "Content Advisor". There is no need to install any apps. Check the following video link for step by step to enable parental control on iPhone devices: https://youtu.be/Lmf9yxwge5Y?si=2rDb_aKSdWHcvTf6

Additional resources exist for managing and overseeing your children's online activity. Several internet service providers offer child protection services. You can read more about these options by contacting your ISP. Alternatively, specialized software can be installed on your computer, each with unique functionalities and attributes, which allow you to choose the best option for your requirements.

2.4 HOW TO PROTECT YOURSELF ONLINE

- Restrict the amount of personal information you share on online platforms – Be careful what personal information you put on social media. Sharing any information might make you vulnerable. For example, don't share your home address or date of birth. In general, pay attention to the sum of the information you post. A skilled attacker could glean enough key facts from your private information to make an educated guess of your password.

- Remember that the internet is accessible to all – The internet is available to everyone with access. Therefore, you should publish only information that you want others to see. Don't upload material or pictures that you don't want to be seen by strangers. Once you publish something, there's no getting it back. Your pictures can be saved on other users' computers. Also, your employer can see everything you post. Both your security and your reputation are at risk. So be careful what you post.

- Be suspicious of strangers – Always be suspicious when you are communicating with strangers. Don't share online information you wouldn't normally share with a stranger. (Some people try to trick you by hiding or giving a false identity. You can never be certain who you are communicating with online.) Set some limitations on what you will put on your profile and who can see it. Change your social media settings to share your profile with only the people you know or your friends. Block some of the information from others and make some available only to yourself.

- Be skeptical. Verify any and all information before taking any further steps. Don't trust everything you see or read online. There are many fake posts created just to trick you. Before acting on it, check the original source of the information

- Evaluate the settings – Most applications offer private settings and generally offer excellent security, thus eliminating the need to maximize your protection. Evaluate and revisit these settings regularly, as the app providers could add valuable new features, or eliminate old, outdated ones. Do not just continue to use the default settings because hackers know how to take advantage of them. Constantly change and customize the settings to your personal needs. Make sure to review and change the list of people who can view your personal information or profile. Finally, make your profile and personal information available only to those you know or want to share it with.

- Be wary of third-party applications – Do not trust any third-party applications and plugins. Use and download applications only from trusted brands and vendors. Don't victimize yourself by downloading a free unverified third-party application that might contain malware or can make your system vulnerable. Third-party applications might be free or provide entertainment or functionality, but they can also be risky or have a payload, so be suspicious when downloading any app whose source you do not know. Furthermore, change the security and privacy settings and limit the amount of data the application can modify or access.

- Use robust passwords – Passwords are the most common way to safeguard your account. But passwords can be compromised, especially if they are not strong enough. Never use a password that can be easily guessed. Your password is the key to your security. Not only can an attacker gain access to your account but, in the event of a compromise, he or she can also impersonate you.

- Be sure to keep your web browser and all software regularly updated. – To keep your system secure, you need to keep it up-to-date. Attackers may find bugs or security holes in your software or system, leaving your data vulnerable to access. Developers regularly provide updates with improvements to add useful new features and patches designed to overcome any security issues. Don't neglect to download them. They will enhance the functionality and security of your system. Be sure to enable auto-update if this option is available; otherwise, you may need to do it manually.

- Use antivirus software – To optimize your security level, you need to set a multi-layer defense. Antivirus software is one layer of protection. This software helps to detect and remove a virus before it can harm or corrupt your system. However, Antivirus cannot remove viruses they are not trained to detect. That's why you must always keep your antivirus up to date. Some viruses, for example, change their signature or shape, making them hard to detect. As a result, it's a good practice to employ more than one countermeasure to protect yourself. We will show you how below.

Chapter 3: Countermeasures

Cyberattacks come in many different forms and functions. Thus, there's no single measure we can take to prevent all attacks. The best we can do is be aware of all the potential areas of vulnerability and understand the strengths and weaknesses of each defense. Being diverse in our defenses is perhaps the most effective strategy. We should focus on the best defense according to the situation. Here are several defenses to consider:

- Encryption
- Minimize Administrator Privileges
- Access control
- Firewall
- Intrusion Detection/Prevention system ID/IP
- Antivirus
- Network Segmentation
- Defense in Depth
- Data Lost Prevention
- Policies and Practices
- Personnel Security

- Biometrics
- Smart cards & tokens
- Auditing / Monitoring
- Physical Security

Most of the time, we need a multi-layer line of defense to mitigate the many different threats. This chapter will introduce you to some of the countermeasures you can implement to protect against the risks covered in the previous chapter.

3.1 PASSWORD MEASURES

- Above all, it's essential to secure your information with a strong password. To make sure your password is robust, follow these key steps:

    1. Make your password long. It should be a minimum of 13 characters. Consider using a passphrase, for they have the dual advantage of being longer yet easier to remember.

    2. Use a combination of letters, digits, and special characters in your password. This increases its complexity, making it harder to guess or crack.

    3. Avoid common words: Using common words makes it easier for attackers to break into your account, especially when

employing a dictionary attack. Be creative; use unique combinations of words.

4. Use a password manager. Password managers store all your passwords for future access, and also help you generate strong, new passwords.

3.2 AUTHENTICATION

- For highly confidential information, you should consider using a multi-tier, or at least a two-tier, authentication. This means that, in addition to the username-password combination, you need to add at least two of the following credentials:

    - Something you know, such as a passcode.

    - Something you are, such as a fingerprint.

    - Something you have, such as a credit card or a key fob.

- Create custom security questions to fortify your defenses. You will be asked one or more security questions if you forget a password. Usually, these questions are standard and preset (what is your mother's maiden name, name of your childhood best friend, what is your favorite movie, etc.). Answers to such questions can sometimes be guessed or inferred based on publicly available information, such as social media. To maximize your security, choose and set your personal questions. Make them so personal that only you know the answer.

- Create separate accounts for each user per device. We highly recommend having more than one account on each device. By creating distinct user accounts, you can limit the privileges of each user. A standard admin account, on the other hand, includes all permissions, which is very risky. A hacker who invades an admin account has unlimited access to the entire system. With separate user accounts, the permissions granted to each user are limited, thus minimizing the potential damage a hacker can cause.

3.3 SECURE NETWORKS

- Be sure to choose secure networks. Avoid using public hotspots as much as possible. Several threats are associated with public Wi-Fi connections, especially if they are unsecured. Using unprotected Wi-fi will potentially expose your transactions and internet traffic to cybercriminals.

- Even if you are connected to password-protected Wi-Fi, you must take extra measures to be fully secure. Public hotspots are common targets of attack. Using a Virtual Private Network service is one way to protect yourself. This will help you to encrypt your incoming and outgoing traffic. However, you still have to be careful because even some encrypted hotspots use an outdated or compromised algorithm. So, you need to be aware of weak algorithms, such as WEP or WPA, and, if possible, use the most recent encryption algorithm.

- Keep all your personal electronic device software current: This step is easy to take and is essential. Outdated software can significantly weaken the security of your system/device. If new patches are offered, use them. They can resolve any issues or security vulnerabilities that might exist in your current version. (They can also add valuable new features that improve your device/system.) Make sure to download any recent updates from the manufacturer's website. Just be sure the downloads are not from any third-party sites, as they are sometimes infected or unreliable.

- Be suspicious of unexpected or unknown emails. One of the most common attacks is phishing emails. Phishing emails look legitimate, but they come from cybercriminals who are trying to gain access to your credentials. Phishing emails contain malicious links or malware that can compromise your system and send your credentials to the attacker. Do not click on or open any email you don't recognize.

3.4 WINDOWS LOGIN PASSWORD POLICY

You can add to or update the user password policy on your Windows computer to manage the policy yourself. For example, you can change the length of the password, the minimum/maximum age of the password, the complexity requirements, etc.

To access these policies, follow these steps:

First, find the search bar on the start menu. Then type the command "*Run* as in Figure 3.1. Next, enter the command "*secpol.msc*", hit enter to open, and use the "Local Security Policy" as in Figure 3.2.

From the left panel, click" Account Policies," then select "*Password Policy*". As in Figure 3.3, you can see the Password Policy settings for configuring. *(Note: security policy "secpol.msc" is not available for Win10 Home Edition)*

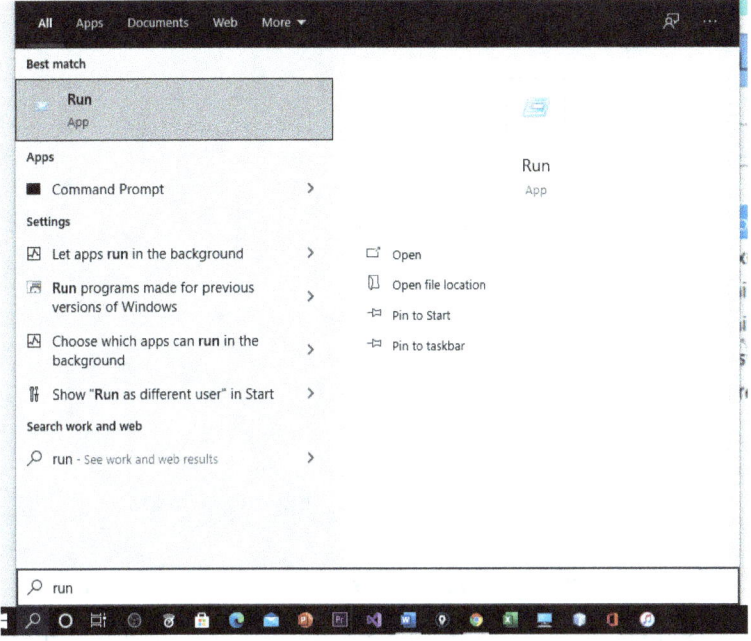

Figure 3.1 Search window

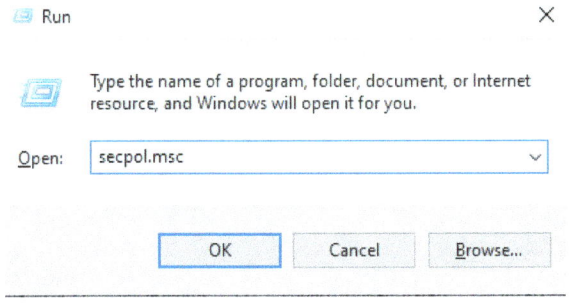

Figure 3.2 Windows Run command

53

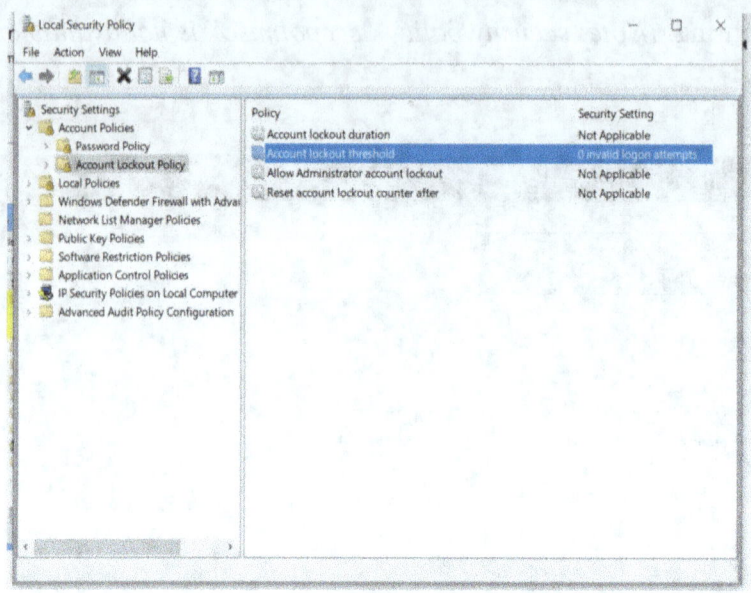

Figure 3.3 Password Policy configuring window.

These are some settings you can configure in order to add to or edit your password policy. You can change these configuration settings by double-clicking each one to open their properties box. As in Figure 3.4, click the drop-down menu to change the password history and choose the desired option. Finally, when you are done, don't forget to click the Apply or OK button to save the settings.

3.4.1 ENFORCE PASSWORD HISTORY

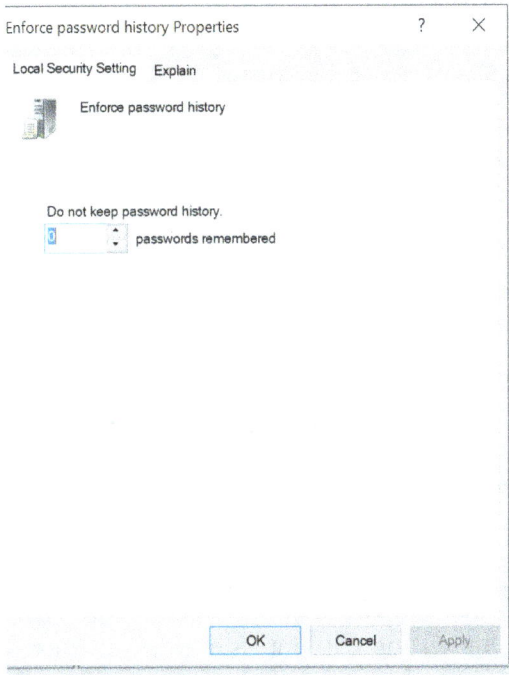

Figure 3.4 Password history properties

The password history settings will help ensure that the users do not repeatedly use old passwords when it's time to create a new one. This setting determines the number of unique passwords you can use before going back to reuse the old one.

The default value is set to 24 on domain controllers and 0 on standalone servers.

3.4.2 MAXIMUM PASSWORD AGE

You can set your password to expire at a date of your choosing. The default age of a password usually is 42 days, but you can set it to expire within the range of 1 to 999 days. (Note: You can also set it to never expire by changing the number of days to zero.)

3.4.3 MINIMUM PASSWORD AGE

The setting for minimum password age forces the user to set a minimum period to use the password before it can be changed. (Age here refers to the age of the password, not the user.) The default value is 0 on standalone servers, which can be between 1 and 998 days. Or you can set it to zero days to allow the user to change the password immediately. This setting will not strengthen the password policy but will prevent users from changing passwords too frequently.

3.4.4 MINIMUM PASSWORD LENGTH

A password can be set between 1 and 14 characters. The default value is 8 characters. For optimum security, we recommend a minimum length of 13 characters. (Note: The default value on domain controllers is 7 characters; on a computer/server, it's 0 characters–meaning no password is required.)

3.4.5 PASSWORD MUST MEET COMPLEXITY REQUIREMENTS.

Figure 3.5 Password complexity

This setting enables you to designate both the minimum requirement for a password and the complexity of the password settings (See Figure 3.5). The password must satisfy all of these requirements when enabling this policy.

Here are the requirements for a strong password:

1. Do not include your full name or account name.

2. The password must be at least 12 characters long and contain three of the following:

    1. Lowercase letters (a - z)
    2. Upper letters (A - Z)
    3. Numbers (0 - 9)
    4. Special characters (!, $, #, %)

3.4.6 STORE PASSWORDS USING REVERSIBLE ENCRYPTION.

Some applications and protocols require the password to be reversible-encrypted and saved as plain text. This setting should never be enabled unless it is required by the applications running on the system. Enabling this setting will make your system vulnerable.

3.5 ACCOUNT LOCKOUT POLICY IN WINDOWS

The Account Lockout is a good countermeasure for brute-force attacks, which try all possible words to find your password. Enabling this setting will limit the number of attempts an attacker can make. After a certain number of attempts, the system will lock up, stopping the attack. To configure these settings, click "Account Lockout Policy" and set the Invalid logins threshold (Figure 3.6).

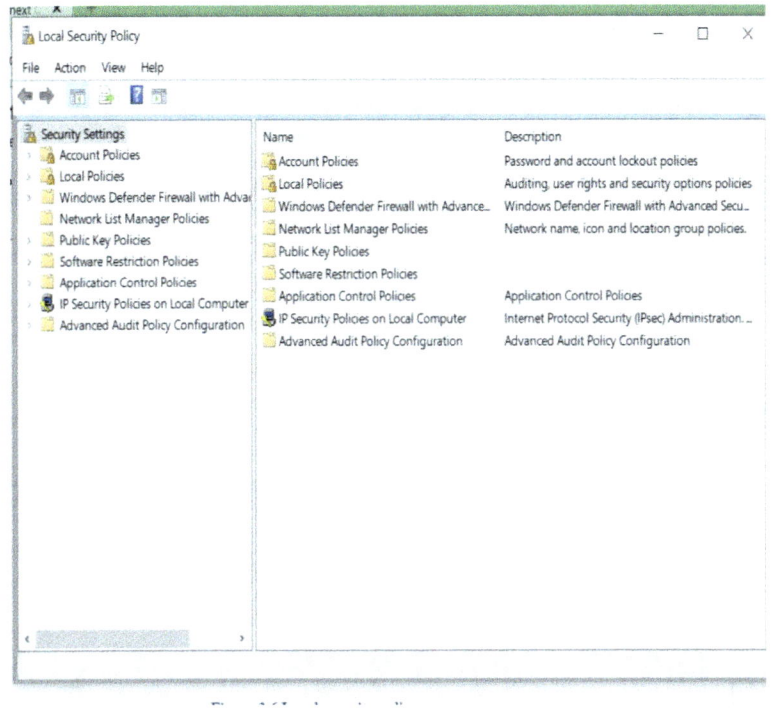

Figure 3.6 Local security policy

3.5.1 ACCOUNT LOCKOUT THRESHOLD FOR INVALID LOGINS

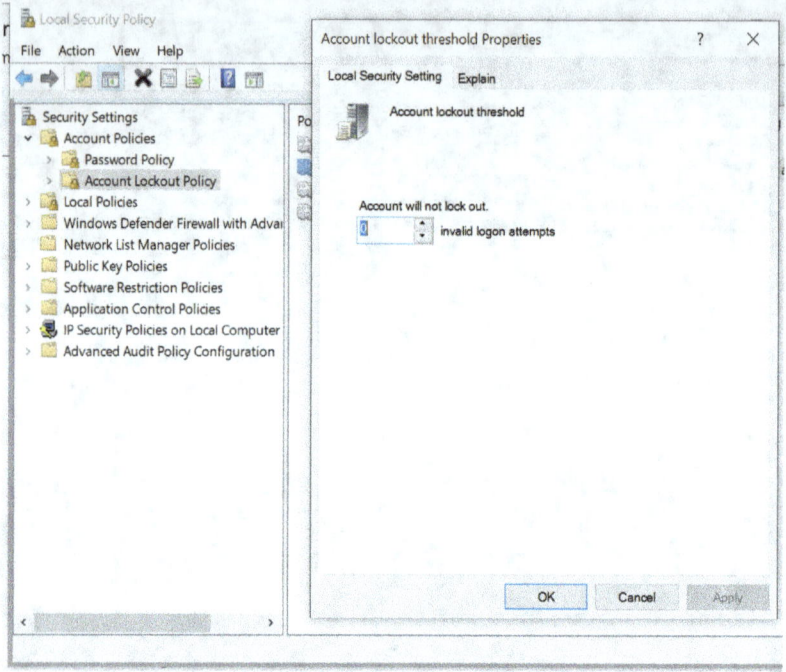

Figure 3.7 Account lockout threshold

Setting this policy allows you to regulate the number of unsuccessful login attempts (Figure 3.7). The initial value is 0, but you can specify a number ranging from 0 to 999 for failed log-on tries.

3.5.2 ACCOUNT LOCKOUT DURATION

You may also need to set the lockout time and the "Account lockout threshold" policy. This way, your account will be locked until you are able to unlock it personally. The lockout duration number can be between 0 and 99.99 minutes.

The policies listed above are settings you can change on Windows to maintain your computer's security. There are many other policies you can apply as well. Take the time to go over these settings and make the correct configurations.

The following sections will focus on other countermeasures you can put in place to secure your apps, software, social media accounts, and others.

3.5.3 ENABLING TWO-STEP AUTHENTICATION ON FACEBOOK

Enabling a two-step authentication will add another layer of defense to your account. This feature is available on most applications, such as email, social media, and others. To enable a two-step authentication, you need to do the following:

Open the Facebook app and click on the Menu button. Then click on the arrow-down icon in the upper right corner, as in the figure below:

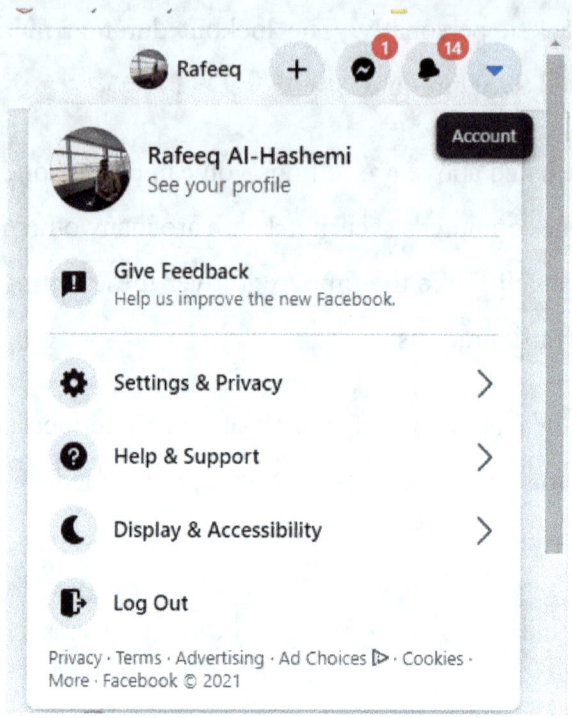

Figure 3.8 Facebook setting

1. To access the Settings & Privacy option, scroll down and click on Settings & Privacy, and then select Security. You will see a listing for the following:

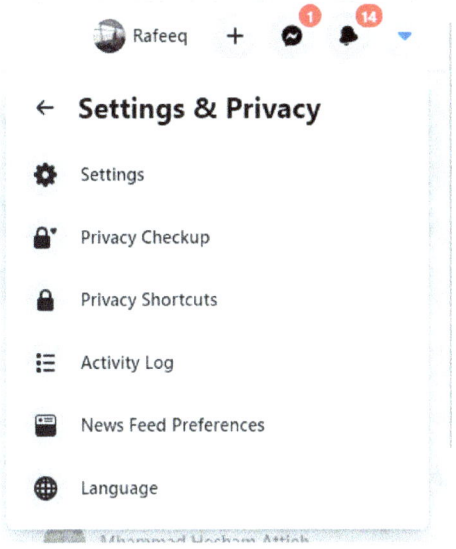

Figure 3.9 Facebook setting & Privacy.

On the left side panel, there's a security and login tab. Click it to see the settings on the right side. Scroll down until you see two-factor authentication settings, as in Figure 3.10.

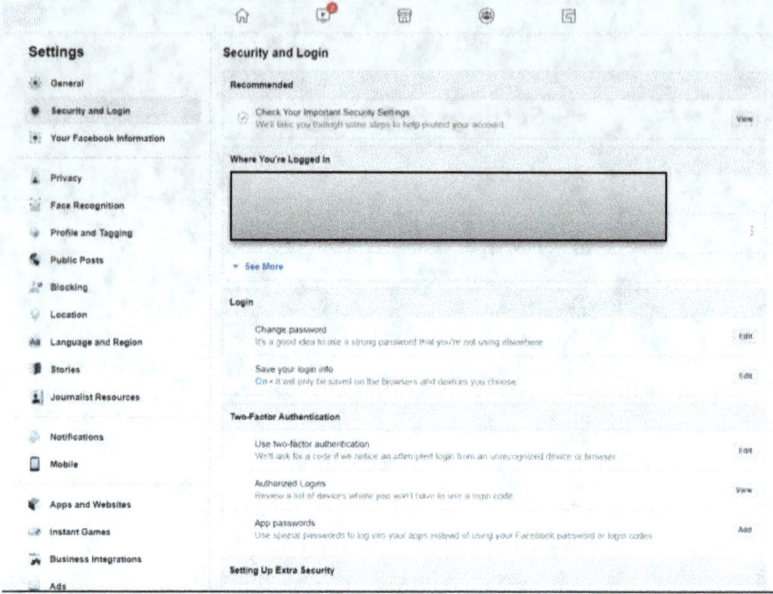

Figure 3.10 Facebook Security and login tab

Click the option "Use Two-Factor Authentication" and select one of the security methods listed in Figure 3.11.

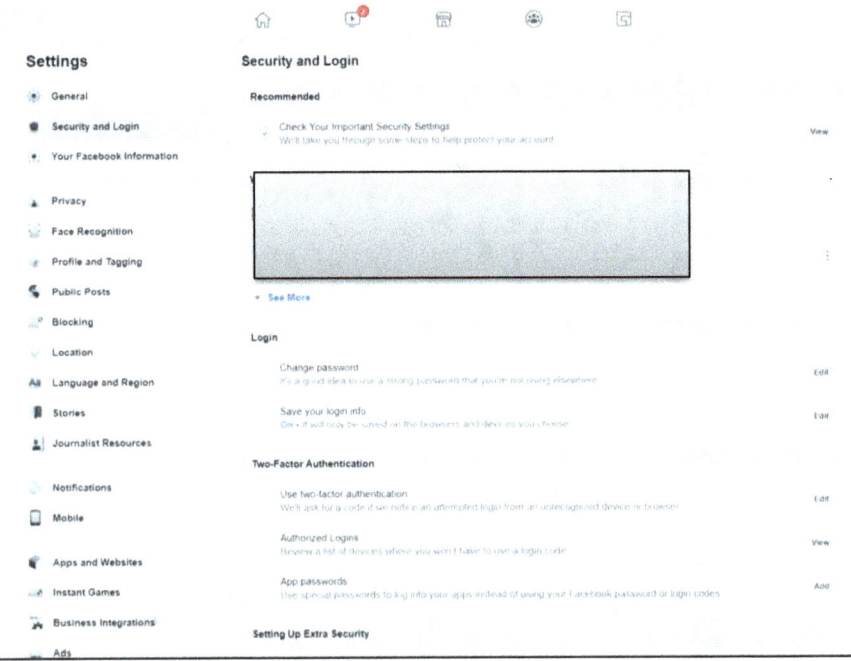

Figure 3.11 Facebook Two-Factor Authentication

To receive a verification code on your phone, click the SMS option, enter your phone number, and follow the instructions, as in Figure 3.12.

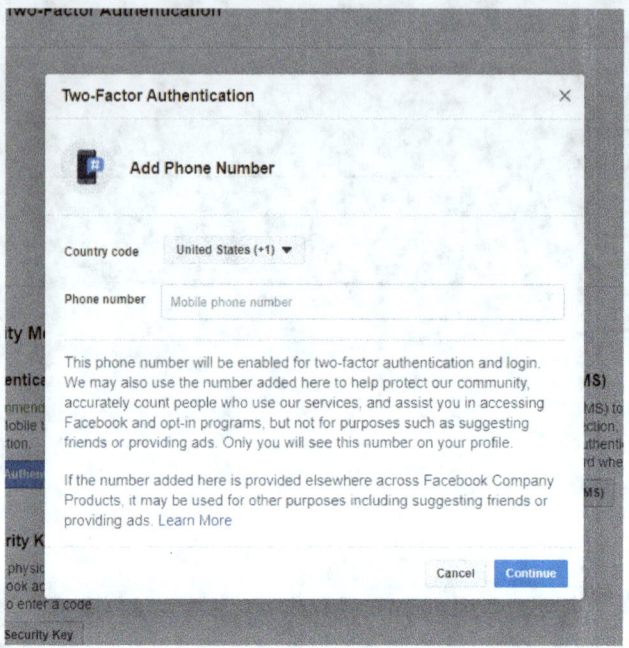

Figure 3.12 Verification code on your phone

We highly recommend taking advantage of two-factor authentication whenever it's offered.

3.6 RECOMMENDED COUNTERMEASURES ON YOUR SMARTPHONE

iPhone devices:

1- Erase all data from your iPhone or iPad before selling your device.

To erase the data on the phone, you need to take the following steps:

These are the steps required for iPhone devices; see Figure 3.13, and Figure 3.14

- Go to the "Settings" app on your iPhone or iPad.
- Go to "General".
- Look down for the "Reset option."
- Choose "Erase All Content and Settings. "
- Also, click on "Erase Reset All settings."
- Click on "Erase iPhone" one more time to confirm.
- Now, write your Passcode.

To complete this process, type your Apple password and turn off the Activate Lock.

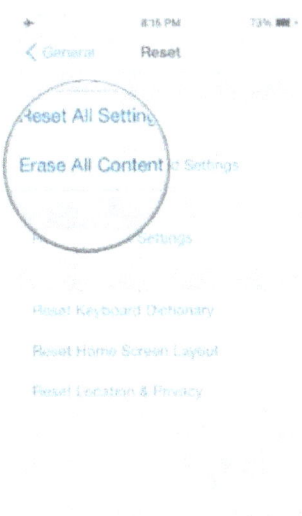

Figure 3.13 Erase All Content and Settings

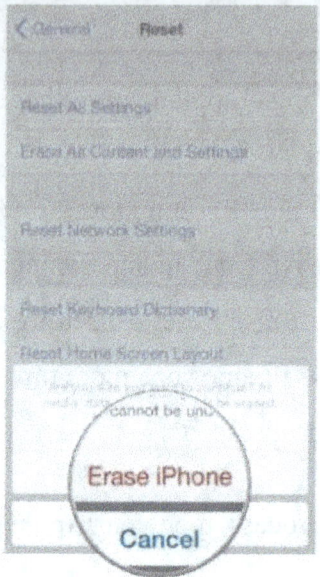

Figure 3.14 Erase iPhone

After completing this process, you can set up a new device, restore it from a stored backup, or sell it to someone.

Be sure to remove all your personal and private information, such as photos, contacts, and any iCloud information, before you sell or give away your device.

The best way to do this is as follows:

1. Unpair your Apple Watch.

2. Make a backup of your device.

3. Log out of your iCloud and iTunes & App Store (this is essential).

4. Go to Settings under your name. Scroll down and select Sign Out. The system will ask you to enter your Apple ID password and select Turn Off.

5. Now you can start deleting and erasing all the data and information on your phone by following the steps listed in the previous section.

6. Upon completion, you can begin deleting.

Here are additional steps you need to take to remove any personal accounts or settings:

1. Sign out and delete your iCloud account. Go to Settings, *select iCloud,* and slide *Off* the *Find My iPhone.*

2. Sign out with Facetime. Go to *Settings,* Facetime, and turn it off; the slider must be grayed out.

Android Devices:

For devices running Android 5.0 Lollipop or a newer version, there is a feature called "Android device protection" or "factory reset protection (FRP)." This feature makes the phone unusable for a new owner if it is reset.  Activation requires the entry of a previously used Google account and password. The FRP feature must be turned off to sell or transfer ownership of the device. Here is how you do it:

Step 1: Disable all screen locks by going to Settings > Security or Lock Screen Security > Screen Lock and changing the type to None.

Step 2: Logout of your Google account and follow these steps to delete it from the device by going to "Settings > Users and Accounts," tapping your account, and then selecting "Remove."

Step 3: For Samsung device owners, it's necessary to eliminate the Samsung account from your phone or tablet.

Step 4: You have the option of carrying out a factory reset. However, this action will only erase data on the application level, while other details, such as SMS and chat messages, may still be retrievable using commonly available data recovery tools.

(Note: if the device uses an older version of Android without FRP, you can skip to step 4.)

To effectively wipe data from your Android device, encrypt it through the Settings menu. No special tools are needed; go to Settings and press the restore option. Note: Devices using Android 6.0 Marshmallow or higher may already be encrypted by default. (Savvides, 2017)

The "7-Pass Erase" feature overwrites free disk space seven times to ensure secure deletion of data. It takes seven times longer than the "Zero Out Data" erase. Additionally, the feature adheres to the DoD 5220.22-M specification, which typically requires three passes but is exceeded by Disk Utility's seven-pass method.

3.7 HOW TO RESIST MALWARE

The best weapon against any cybersecurity threat is education. You must educate yourself, your family, and your friends to know the most common cybersecurity threats and how best to mitigate them. You need to know what malware is (in all its variations) and how to protect yourself from it. In addition, you should know what to do in case you get infected with it. The previous chapter covered most of the malware types. Here are some easy steps you can take to mitigate your risks:

Data Backups. Keep a backup of your system and the essential files on your device. If your data is valuable or sensitive, we recommend that you make multiple copies of the backup and store them in different locations. We highly recommend that you create backups frequently. Everyone's needs are different. For some people, backing up once a month is adequate. It depends on how much you use your computer or access your files.

Your backups must be stored on a separate external Hard Disk Drive. Make sure to check these copies occasionally, and also, be sure you are able to access and restore your files without problems.

- Access control. One way to avoid becoming a victim of malware is to implement access control restrictions on your files. This helps prevent bad actors from accessing and modifying your code without your permission. The forthcoming chapter will cover some steps you can take to add access control restrictions to your device.

- Restrict administrative access. Doing this adds another layer of protection by preventing any malware from accessing the admin account. This is critical because access to the admin account gives bad actors access to your entire system. Using a default user account is one of the best ways to limit access to your system. This way, if ransomware or other malware infects your system, the harm it can inflict is limited. (Please refer to the previous chapter for background.) More details on this point are available in the next chapter.

- Software Update. It's essential to keep your software, system, and antivirus up to date. This will mitigate the risk of malware in general and ransomware in particular. Activate auto-update, if available, and don't fail to patch the software with any new updates. This will fortify any known vulnerabilities the ransomware could utilize to gain entry into your system.

3.8 RANSOMWARE SYSTEM-LEVEL PROTECTION

It's challenging to prevent or block ransomware, especially at the most common entry points, such as emails and websites. One of the most effective steps is installing anti-malware to check your emails and block any ransomware. Not all antiviruses provide this feature, however. You must install one that can scan your computer's emails and files. Also, remember that up-to-date anti-malware/Antivirus software is not guaranteed to detect the latest malware/ransomware.

For optimum email protection, consider the following practices:

- Filtering emails: Filtering is one of the best practices you can employ to safeguard your email. Filtering helps limit the number of spam emails and emails that contain malicious attacks.

- Blocking attachments: To reduce the potential attack area, block email attachments. Most malware, especially Ransomware, is delivered as an executable attachment to an email. Malware can be in the form of direct executables, Microsoft Office files that contain macros, or zip/rar files. Therefore, it's essential to have a policy in place that requires an email security appliance, or some antivirus/anti-malware software that removes email attachments.

  o We recommend that you review permission-related practices Doing so can greatly reduce the impact of a ransomware attack.

Removing local administrative privileges: Local administrative privileges, when breached, allow ransomware attackers to control and modify system files, directories, registries, and storage. Removing local administrative privileges will block access to these critical areas, which are often targeted for encryption by ransomware attackers.

o Limit permissions access: Ransomware needs access permission to modify your files, so limiting access to your most sensitive files and directories is essential. It's also imperative to ensure that predefined applications–known as a whitelist–have a right-to-access to your files/system. Many users/organizations do business using a limited set of applications. By limiting permission access, you are blocking applications that are not on the whitelist, including ransomware.

- Also, logging in at specific access points, such as local drives, could prevent ransomware from spreading and causing harm.

3.9 RANSOMWARE NETWORK-LEVEL PROTECTION

- Preventing the spread of ransomware has become increasingly difficult, particularly with respect to networks. Firewalls that use whitelisting or strong blacklisting techniques can prevent downloads of web-based malware and can make it more difficult for ransomware to connect with command-and-control servers.

- One of the most effective ways to curb ransomware is to completely block all remote services, including remote desktop protocol (RDP). Spam detection strategies, such as spam lists, can also help. Another tactic is to limit the types of file extensions allowed to be sent via email.

- One of the keys to preventing the spread of ransomware in a network is to protect the internal host computer. The most efficient way to do this is to disconnect the host: in other words, literally remove the wired connections, the Wi-Fi, and the Bluetooth connections. Also, don't forget to turn off the automated backups to both local and external storage.

3.10 MEASURES IN THE EVENT OF A RANSOMWARE ATTACK

○ Protecting your organization entirely from ransomware is not possible. If you are the victim to a ransomware attack, we recommend that you take the following measures.

○ Before shutting down your system, take a photo of the screen. It may help to identify the kind of ransomware used to attack you later. Also, try to keep any cryptographic data you can gather. This kind of information could help you to decrypt your data later.

○ Shutdown your computer to prevent the ransomware from spreading and causing more damage to your data. This should be done on the affected system.

- To prevent the ransomware attack from spreading, it's imperative to determine the path and methods that the attacker is using (this is what is called an attack vector) and retrieve any emails suspected of carrying out the attack.

- You must block the ransomware's command-and-control server from gaining access to your data. Once the ransomware gains access to your data, it's too late: it will encrypt it. Thus, if you can block the ransomware server, you are likely to succeed in blocking the attack.

We recommend informing the authorities about any ransomware incident, as they can aid in the investigation. However, it's important to note that each countermeasure comes with a cost. Involving law enforcement may prolong the recovery process, and the longer one waits to pay the ransom, generally the higher the ransom payment becomes. Still, we stand by our recommendation. Although doing so could result in a higher payment, the most prudent way to proceed is to include the authorities.

3.11   Wrapping Up and Looking Ahead

Ransomware has become both more prevalent and more profitable. As a result, ransomware criminals have increasingly focused on large organizations, such as government entities, educational institutions, and healthcare providers. Ransomware is a low-risk, high-return criminal business that offers the added benefit of anonymity. As a result, we can expect that ransomware criminals will continue to develop increasingly more sophisticated technology in the future.

While law enforcement and government entities continue to address ransomware attacks, maintaining best practices can help protect your organization or mitigate the damage. (Ransomware: Best Practices for Prevention and Response, 2017)

3.12 SECURITY TIP

3.12.1 EVALUATING YOUR WEB BROWSER'S SECURITY SETTINGS

To ensure maximum security, check your web browser settings and confirm that they are set at the appropriate level. Increasing your security settings may reduce the functionality of some websites, but the tightened security is generally worth the inconvenience.

3.12.2 THE SIGNIFICANCE OF SECURITY SETTINGS FOR WEB BROWSERS

Security configurations for web browsers are important because your web browser is your computer's main gateway to the Internet. Moreover, different applications may depend on your browser (or its elements) to operate properly. Hence, your browser's security settings are critical. Web applications may aim to improve your browsing experience by offering different features, but this can potentially leave you vulnerable to attacks. To mitigate such a risk, turn off all unnecessary settings. Once you confirm that a website is trustworthy, you may temporarily enable the functionality, but we recommend that you disable it once you're done browsing the site.

3.12.3 WHERE CAN YOU FIND THE SETTINGS?

The security options in web browsers vary; therefore, locating them may require some effort. For instance, in Internet Explorer, you can navigate to the (Security) tab by clicking on (Tools) in the menu bar, choosing Internet (Options...), and then selecting (Custom Level...).

In Firefox, click on (Tools) in the menu bar and select (Options...). Afterward, you can explore the basic security options by clicking on the (Content, Privacy, and Security) tabs.

Since security options and configurations vary by browser, you may need to check the help feature or refer to the vendor's website in order to familiarize yourself with them.

Applications have preset or default settings. Your browser may also have predetermined security levels from which you can choose. For instance, Internet Explorer provides customized settings that enable you to choose a specific security level, which then activates or deactivates certain features based on your selection.

Even though these guidelines are available, it's still advisable to familiarize yourself with the various terminologies to help you evaluate the features and determine which settings best suit your needs.

3.12.4 How do you know what your settings should be

The most ideal practice is to configure your security settings to the highest level available. However, it's essential to note that certain features may not work correctly or may not load if you restrict them. We recommend enabling features only when needed and always maintaining the highest level of security possible.

3.12.5 What do the different terms mean

Various web browsers use their own distinct terminology; however, the subsequent terms and alternatives are generally utilized industrywide.

Your web browser may be able to categorize websites into distinct zones and permit the establishment of various security limitations for each zone.

Internet Explorer identifies the following zones:

- The Internet serves as a common space for all websites that can be accessed. The security measures for each site are automatically activated when you visit it. To ensure the best possible protection during your browsing activities, we advise setting the security level to the highest level or at least to the medium level.

- Local intranet - A local intranet is a private network in which an organization's server is used primarily to share information and perform work-related tasks with internal members or employees. It's generally safe to maintain less stringent settings for local intranets. But there have been instances where viruses have managed to gain access to this platform, so it's crucial to check and identify which websites are listed, and the permissions granted to each.

- Trusted sites - You must be careful about which sites you add to your trusted list. If you believe a website prioritizes security and has trustworthy content, add it to your trusted zone. You can set the configurations so that only websites with the "Secure Sockets Layer (SSL)" protocol are active in this zone. Note: You should still set the security level to "high," even though you trust an external site, as it could be vulnerable to attacks that could affect you.

- Restricted sites - It's crucial to realize that relying solely on security configurations is not enough. To ensure complete protection and to enhance security, users can identify potentially unsafe websites and modify their settings accordingly. Nevertheless, the most secure approach is to avoid completely visiting websites whose safety you have doubts about.

- JavaScript - JavaScript is used by certain websites to achieve a desired look or functionality, but you should be aware that JavaScript can also be used for malicious purposes.

- Plug-ins - Plug-ins are used to customize your browser. They are especially useful in adding functionality. Java and ActiveX are two of the most popular plug-ins. It's important to remember that plug-ins are vulnerable to attack too, including cyberattack. Don't install any plug-ins unless necessary; if you do install them, be sure they come from a reliable site.

Here are some other security measures you may need to implement:

- Manage cookies - One can choose to disable, restrict, or permit cookies as needed. In most cases, disabling cookies is the most prudent way to proceed. They can be enabled later for trusted websites that require them.

- Block pop-up windows - This will reduce the number of pop-up ads you receive, which is important because some pop-ups could be harmful. However, you should know that activating this feature may limit the functionality of some websites. (Rafail, n.d.)

3.13 HOW TO MINIMIZE THE RISKS TO YOUR WIRELESS NET

- Change the default password - Network devices, including wireless access points, are often given default passwords during set-up. However, such passwords are generally weak and thus are vulnerable to attack. You should change the default to a strong password and update it regularly.

- Restrict access - It's important to be able to filter out any addresses that might pose a threat to your network. Media access control (MAC) allows you to do this. MAC grants access to known and authorized devices while blocking addresses you don't know or do not want to connect to your hardware. Also, consider creating a "guest" account. Such accounts are available on many wireless routers. They provide guests access on a separate channel using a unique password. This will help you keep your sensitive login details confidential.

- Encrypt the data on your network - To safeguard your network from unauthorized access, it's essential to encrypt the data transmitted over your wireless connection. Several encryption protocols are available, including Wired Equivalent Privacy (WEP), Wi-Fi Protected Access (WPA), WPA2, and WPA3. These protocols offer different methods for encrypting data between wireless routers and devices. WEP and WPA are weak encryption algorithms, but WPA3 is considered the most reliable encryption option. So, in order to ensure the highest level of security for your network, we recommend using equipment that supports WPA3.

- Protect your Service Set Identifier (SSID) - We recommend that you not share your SSID in any public format. All Wi-Fi routers offer an option to change your SSID to a unique identity, which makes it more difficult for thieves to steal. We recommend using that option. In fact, doing so is the minimum step you should take. If you fail to do it, you are exposing yourself to potential attackers who can break into the router.

- Install a firewall - We recommend installing a firewall on your router, modem, and home network. Although it's possible for attackers to bypass a firewall, this extra step makes it more difficult for them.

- Maintain antivirus software - To ensure the security of your device, it's imperative that you install antivirus software and regularly update your virus definitions. Certain antivirus programs have special features that can identify and safeguard against Spyware and adware.

- Use file sharing with caution - When file sharing is not needed, we recommend disabling it. Also, we recommend restricting file sharing only to home or work networks. Never allow file-sharing on public networks. We also recommend establishing a specific folder for file-sharing purposes in order to prevent access to all other directories. It's crucial to password-protect any shared material. It's also critical to avoid sharing an entire hard drive.

- Keep your access point software patched and up to date - Your wireless access point manufacturer will regularly issue updates and patches for its software and firmware. It's essential to frequently check the manufacturer's website for updates or patches that are specific to your device, and to update and patch accordingly.

- Check your Internet provider's or router manufacturer's wireless security options - To enhance the security of your wireless network, we recommend consulting the customer support section of your Internet service provider, and the router manufacturer's website for guidance and materials on security enhancements.

- Use a virtual private network to secure your connection - Many companies and organizations make use of a virtual private network (VPN), which allows their employees to securely connect to their network from outside the office. VPNs encrypt both the sending and the receiving end of the connections and block unencrypted traffic. If you have access to a VPN, be sure to log in whenever you use a public wireless access point. (Securing Wireless Networks, 2023)

3.14 How To Enable Two-Factor Authentication On Gmail And Google

Google offers the option of activating 2FA for your Gmail account through its centralized settings page. Once enabled, these enhanced security settings will also be applied to other Google services, such as Google Drive and Google+. Despite Google labeling it as "two-step verification," the underlying concept remains the same. You will be able to further enhance your security by requesting both something you possess (such as your phone) and something you know (such as your password) during the sign-in process.

1. Clicking on the upper-right corner of your profile picture (Figure 3.15) will allow you access to your account settings. Then click "My Account," then click "Sign-in & Security," per Figure 3.16, below:

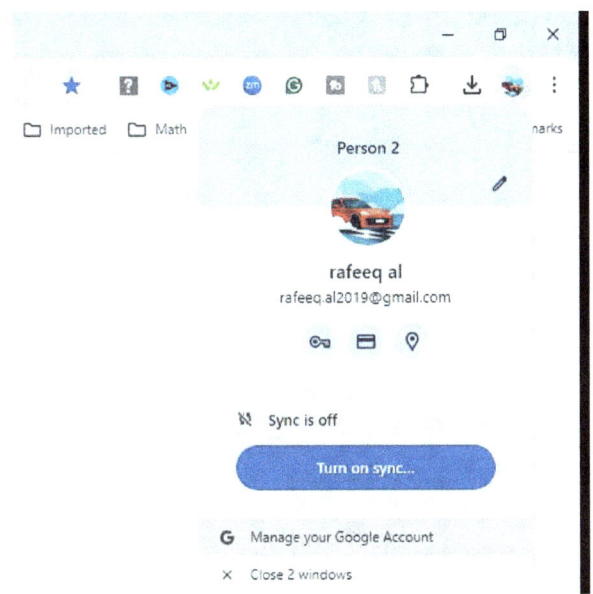

Figure 3.15 Google profile settings

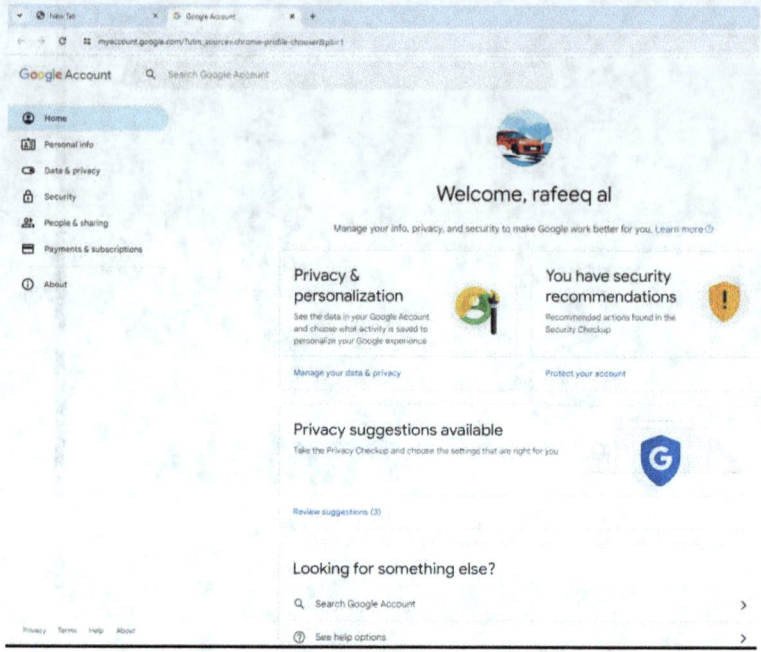

Figure 3.16 Google My Account settings.

2. To activate the "2-Step Verification" feature, go to the section titled "Security" on the left side panel and follow the instructions.

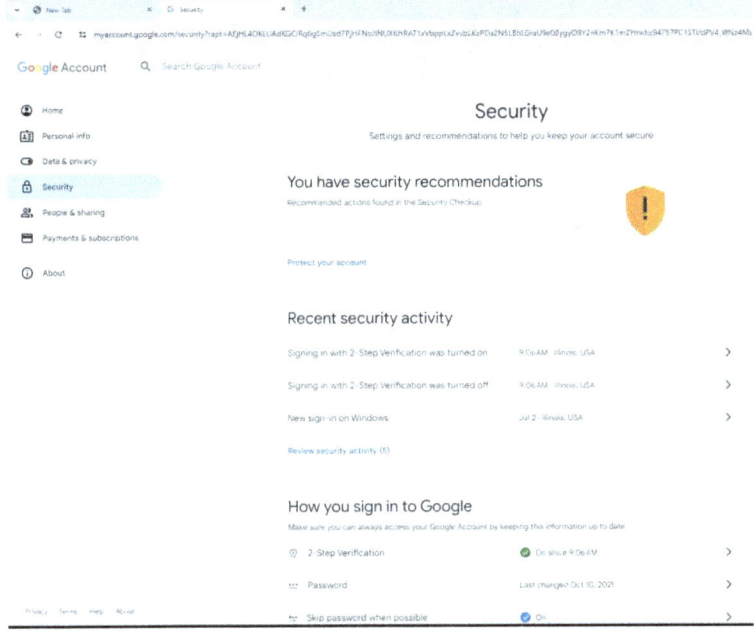

Figure 3.17 Google 2-step verification

3. You may be required to re-enter your password and log in again before you can update your login details.

4. If you want to enable two-factor authentication, click on the "2-step verification" as shown in the figure 3.17 and figure 3.18.

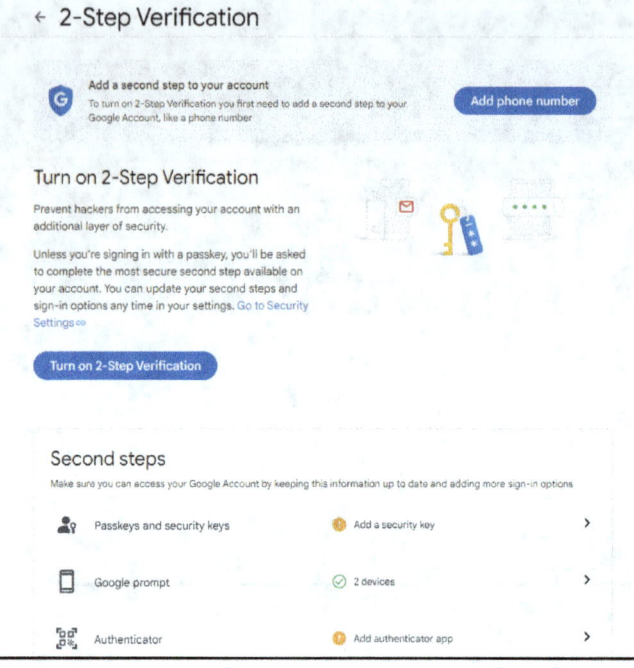

Figure 3.18 2-step verification activation

5. Enter your cell phone number so that you can receive text messages and/or phone calls on this number.

6. You will then receive a code through a text message or phone call. Simply input the numerical digits without the "G-" prefix and select the "Next" option. For visual guidance, please consult Figure 3.19 and 3.20.

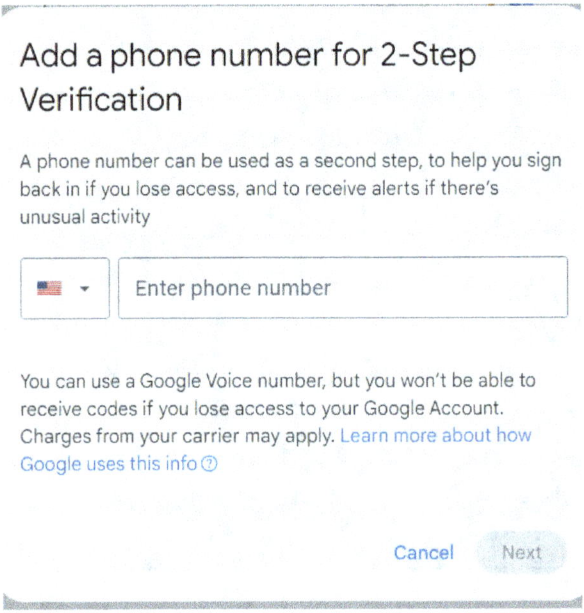

Add a phone number for 2-Step Verification

A phone number can be used as a second step, to help you sign back in if you lose access, and to receive alerts if there's unusual activity

[🇺🇸 ▼] Enter phone number

You can use a Google Voice number, but you won't be able to receive codes if you lose access to your Google Account. Charges from your carrier may apply. Learn more about how Google uses this info ⓘ

Cancel   Next

Figure 3.19 Adding a phone number

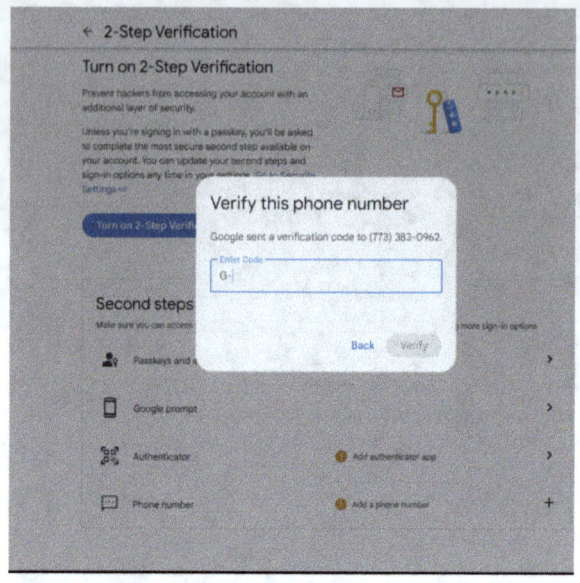

Figure 3.20 Verification code

7. The 2-step authentication feature will be Turned on, as in the following figure

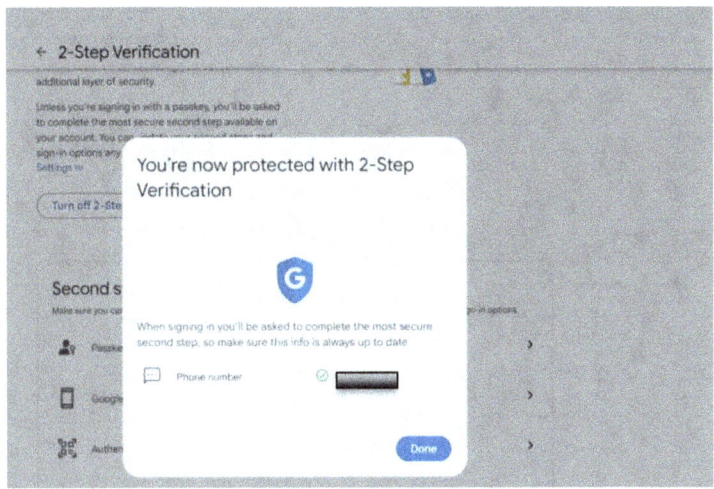

Figure 3.21 Turn on 2-step Verification.

Upon revisiting Google's 2-Step Verification settings page, you have the option to set up an alternate second factor in case you are unable to receive text messages or phone calls. It is crucial to understand that SMS codes can be intercepted, making them less secure compared to other methods. Google's Authenticator app is a reliable and freeway option that generates single-use passwords. It's compatible with various platforms like Facebook, Dropbox, and Microsoft.

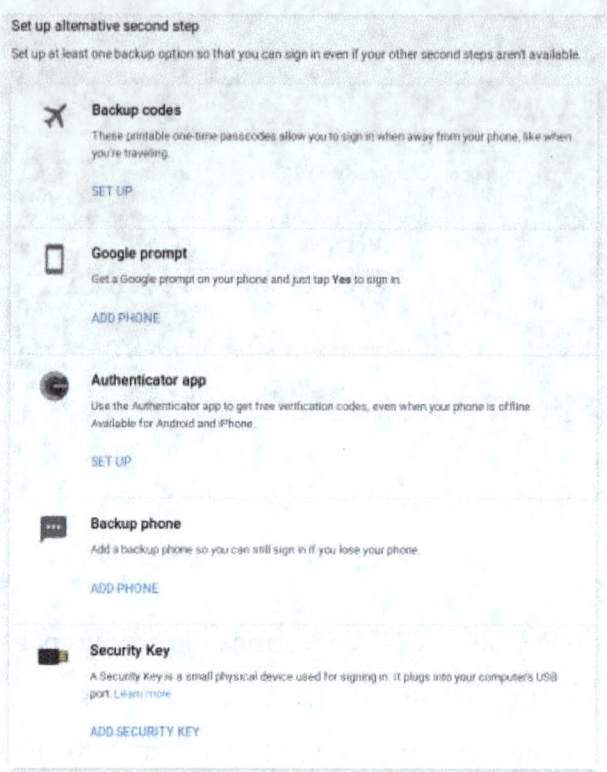

Figure 3.22

In order to access your Gmail on third-party devices or applications, it's important to create app passwords. An app password is a passcode of 16 digits that gives an app or device permission to access your Google Account. App passwords are necessary for devices and applications that do not allow you to log in using a one-time verification code. Typically, the verification process requires you to enter and verify an app password just one time for each app or device. (GEBHART, 2016)

3.15 TIPS THAT CAN HELP AVOID A SPYWARE ATTACK

1. Disable the autorun feature

We recommend that you turn off the autorun on your system. If enabled, malware (such as Trojan horses, Worms, Spyware, etc.) could be installed when you plug in a USB device.

2. Be wary of free adware

A wide range of free software is available on the internet. It's easy to locate software suitable for various tasks. Although certain programs can be useful, it's difficult to determine if they have malicious code embedded in them. Even seemingly harmless software might have been created with the intention of monitoring your activities. It's important to thoroughly research the origin of any software before granting it permission to make changes to your computer.

3. Beware of pop-up ads, especially unwanted ones and those shouting about awards

Online advertisements pop up on your screen all the time. Do not open them. Don't even click any buttons labeled "Cancel" or "Close." Instead, right-click on the window border at the top and choose "Close."

4. If you receive an email with an attachment from an unknown sender, never download it.

Be wary of any links or attachments, particularly in emails that are unexpected or whose sender you don't recognize. This is good practice even with emails that appear to be from a known source. Always verify the URL before opening any link or attachment. Typing it into your internet browser is the safest way to do this.

5. Get Browser Sandbox protection

Browser sandbox offers an added layer of protection by creating a virtual environment around your internet browser. With the sandbox, files that are downloaded or accessed through the browser are blocked from gaining access to your computer and therefore cannot cause harm.

6. Turn ON the popup blocker

Blocking popup ads is a straightforward task. Just use the popup blocker function in your browser. However, keep in mind that certain websites rely on popups for specific purposes. As a result, it might be necessary to disable this feature for websites you trust.

7. Keep the OS and other software up to date

An old operating system or outdated software is vulnerable to cyber-crime. They can make for easy entry points for cybercriminals seeking to gain access to your computer. Such software may contain weaknesses that hackers can easily exploit by installing spyware and other malware on your device.

8. Use a multilayered antivirus solution

Today's malware is far superior to past versions. Attackers have developed more subtle, versatile, and destructive ways of attacking you. As a result, conventional antivirus software is inadequate. Today, your antivirus software contains both sandbox and web protection that guards against fraudulent and infected websites. Of course, the best antivirus software is the one that will block not only current spyware and other malware but malicious code that hasn't even been developed yet.

3.16 HOW TO DETECT SPYWARE

If your computer runs slowly, it could be an indication of the presence of malware. In some cases, a slow computer could result in your being automatically redirected to a suspicious website. The following occurrences could be an indication of such malware:

- The continuous appearance of pop-up windows.

- The website automatically redirects you to other websites.

- Error messages from Windows appear randomly.

- The computer's performance suddenly slowed down.

- Unexpected toolbars suddenly appear in the web browser.

- Unrecognized new icons appear in the taskbar.

- The home page of your browser has changed suddenly. (Tomar, 2014)

Homepage Hijacking

Upon opening your internet browser, you may discover an unfamiliar homepage. Additionally, you might find that the ability to customize your browser settings has been restricted and that your "Favorites" folder has been altered.

Redirected Web Searches

If you are searching for something and an unauthorized browser appears and finishes the search, or if you attempt to delete something and it promptly comes back, these are indications that you've been infected with spyware.

Performance Problems

Your computer's connection speed has decreased and frequently freezes or crashes. This happens because spyware programs run in the background and use up valuable disk space, which can lead to major speed and performance issues.

INUNDATION OF POP-UP ADS

Pop-up ads constantly appear on your screen, even when you're offline. Some of these ads may even be customized with your name.

EXPENSIVE PHONE BILLS

Certain spyware programs can make calls to 1-900 numbers through both broadband and dial-up lines via your computer.

OVERLY ACTIVE MODEM ACTIVITY

Blinking modem lights may indicate excessive web browsing, downloading, or other activity, even if you are not online. Spyware programs frequently transmit and receive data through your computer without your knowledge.

FILES MYSTERIOUSLY CHANGE

Your computer files appear, move, or disappear without warning. Also, the icons on your desktop and toolbars may be blank or absent.

3.16.1   CD TRAY WITH A MIND OF ITS OWN

The drawer of your CD is opening and closing on its own.

Unidentified sent emails

There are emails present in your sent folder that you did not send. (BIS, 2023)

Users and system administrators must take specific steps to prevent viruses from infecting their computing devices. Always proceed cautiously when opening email attachments or running programs. Install and regularly update the newest versions of antivirus software. Also, remember that stealth and polymorphic viruses are especially challenging to antivirus software, as they conceal themselves and can change their form.

3.17 Trojan Horse Prevention

- The surest way to prevent Trojan Horse software from infecting your computer is the simplest, most conservative way: never run any software whose origin, security, or integrity you cannot verify.

- Another way to block a Trojan Horse is to keep a virus-checking program running on the system.

3.18 How do you recognize a sniffer?

Sniffers are especially challenging because they operate surreptitiously and, therefore, can be extremely hard to detect, particularly for the average user. The best way to defend against Sniffers is to use anti-sniffer or other internet security software. One could also use their own sniffer program to detect outside sniffers, but generally speaking, standard anti-sniffer software (or similar security programs) should be adequate to eliminate most risks.

3.18.1 SNIFFEER REMOVAL PROCEDURE

Eradicating sniffer malware that has infected your system can be very challenging. If you discover you are infected, you will need to utilize a robust antivirus program. However, to fully ensure your computer is clean, you must delete all your related files and folders. If the sniffer is on your network, we recommend using software that employs a scanner. Scanners not only find sniffer programs within a network, but they also offer instructions on how to eliminate sniffer malware.

3.18.2 HOW TO PREVENT SNIFFER

There are three steps you should take to prevent a sniffer attack: First, be sure all your communication, both sent and received, is encrypted. Second, scan your network regularly to search for any embedded threats. Third, use only Wi-Fi networks you are confident you can trust.

3.18.3   HOW TO PROTECT YOURSELF FROM A SNIFFER

A good way to protect yourself against a sniffer is to use robust antivirus software, such as Avast Free. However, encrypting all sensitive transmissions, including email, is the most effective protection. You can achieve complete security on any network by encrypting all digital communications using Avast Secure Line. (Belcic, 2020)

3.19 ARTIFICIAL INTELLIGENCE AND CYBERSECURITY:

Today, cyberattacks are so frequent and sophisticated that it's hard to keep up our defenses. Perhaps the most effective protection available today is Artificial Intelligence (AI). AI provides both a pro-active and a self-learning defense system. Utilizing specially designed algorithms, it can identify abnormalities in network traffic or system configuration that could be indicative of an attack. AI's pro-active defense, particularly Artificial Neural Networks (ANN), recognizes changes in data transmission by comparing the current transmission to past transmissions. AI also can assess vulnerabilities and conduct penetration testing, increasing the chances of heading off threats before they do damage.

3.19.1 ADVANCED MALWARE DETECTION

AI-based antivirus software is far superior to today's common signature-based software. Through the use of behavioral analysis, self-discovery, and self-learning techniques, AI can detect new and unfamiliar malware. Moreover, AI's discovery is both faster and more accurate than current antivirus software.

3.20 AI CYBERSECURITY COUNTERMEASURES

In the first nine months of 2021, there were 495 million ransomware attacks globally, an increase of 148% over the previous year. The sheer number of attacks shows how critical AI is to the future of our security. With the current technology, we lack the bandwidth to analyze or control such a high volume of attacks. AI, however, has the necessary bandwidth. It uses algorithms called machine learning that can predict and, in some cases, prevent future attacks. It has proven especially effective in detecting changes in computer behavior and internet traffic, which could be an indication of malicious activity. In general, AI will continue to be a great step forward in cyber protection, as it enables earlier, more accurate, and swifter detection.

3.21 TOP 7 CYBER SECURITY TOOLS THAT USE AI

- Darktrace Antigena

  This is a self-learning AI tool to stop attacks. It's so fast, it can prevent attacks from occurring in real time. It identifies abnormal behaviors and takes immediate action.

- WP Hacked Help (WPHH)

  WordPress is a content management system (CMS) and is a frequent target of cyberattacks. WPHH is a WordPress security service that secures and recovers WordPress websites. There is also an AI-based tool for malware scanners.

- bioHAIFCS

  This is a high-level security framework used to protect critical networks.

- Cognito by Vectra

  Cognito uses AI-driven detection techniques to quickly identify, prioritize, and stop attacks within the Cloud, IoT, and networks.

- DefPloreX Targeted Attack Analytics (TAA) by Symantec is a toolkit that uses Machine Learning algorithms to identify large scale cybercrimes.

CHAPTER 4: BEST PRACTICES

In this chapter, we will cover best cyber practices to help you mitigate your risks and protect your assets from evolving cyberthreats. We will look at encryption mechanisms, and discuss maintaining backups, keeping your OS up to date, creating strong and unique passwords, and choosing effective antiviruses. We will also look at the most effective ways to protect your network and internet connection, including employing secure firewall configurations and creating network monitoring strategies that prevent data breaches. We will also explore ways to improve security and safeguard the privacy of your personal information through such methods as adjusting the security and privacy settings, scrutinizing third-party plugins and software, as well as taking the proper precautions when engaging in an online activity.

Following the practices covered in this chapter and all the information provided to you in this book will help you to establish a formidable system of defense to work confidently in the cyber world.

3.22 OPERATING SYSTEM:

- Create and use a user account in Windows/OS instead of the admin account.

- Encrypt your hard drive.

- Make a backup of your essential/sensitive information on an offline HDD.

- Use a complex password. Passwords can be complex and easy to memorize. See the recommendations listed above.

- Change the default settings.

- Set/Activate OS policies, such as the Password policy.

- Turn the computer off completely. It's not good practice to let your computer sleep or hibernate.

- Use screen privacy protection for your laptop.

- Disable/delete all unneeded services and applications.

- Disable USB/FDD if not needed (Removable media)
  1. Go to the Control Panel

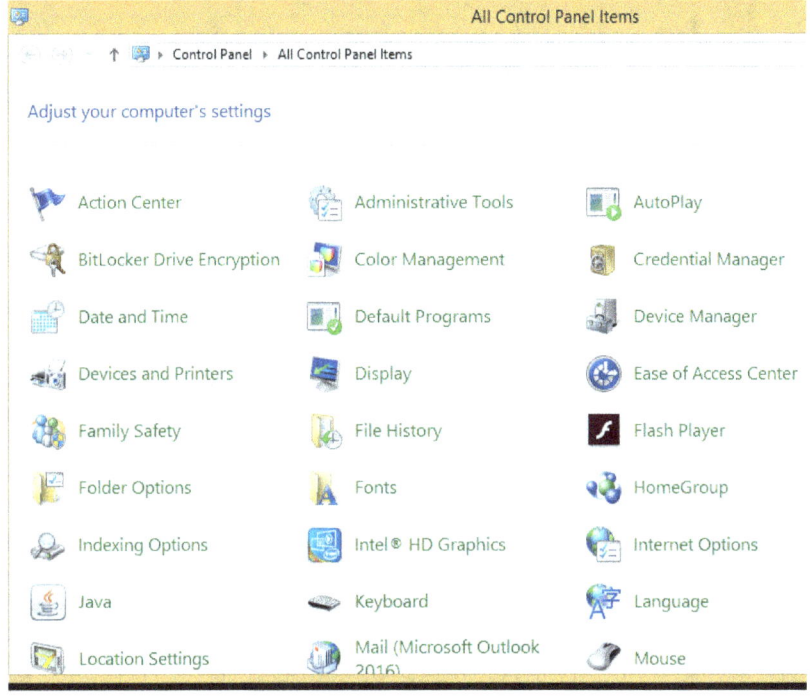

Figure 4.1 Control panel

2. Go to Local Computer Policy

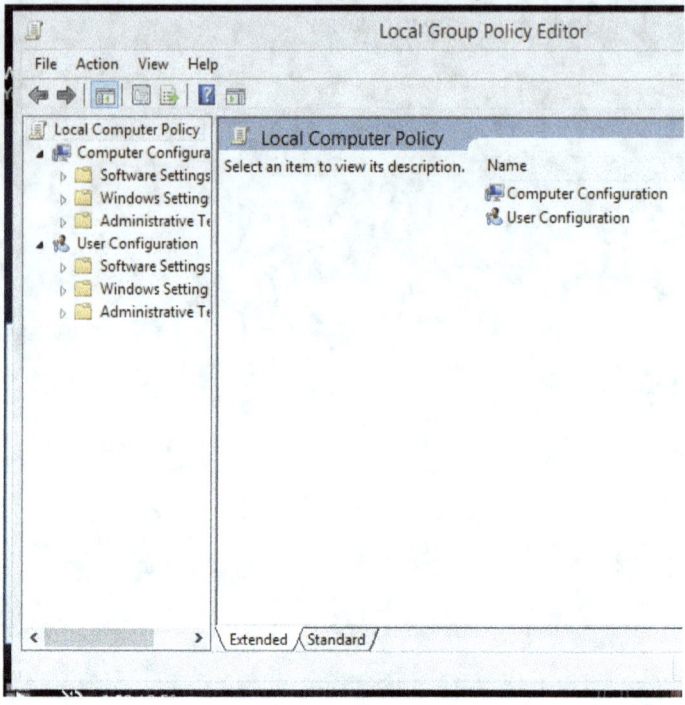

Figure 4.2 Computer policy

3. Select Admin Temp

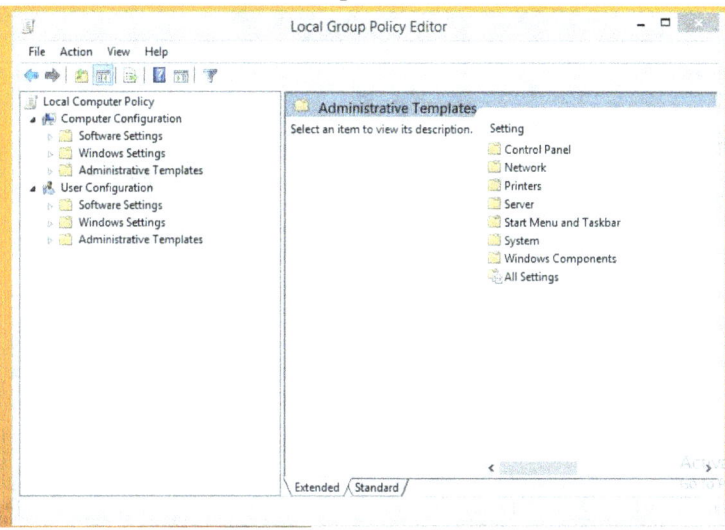

Figure 4.3 Admin Templates

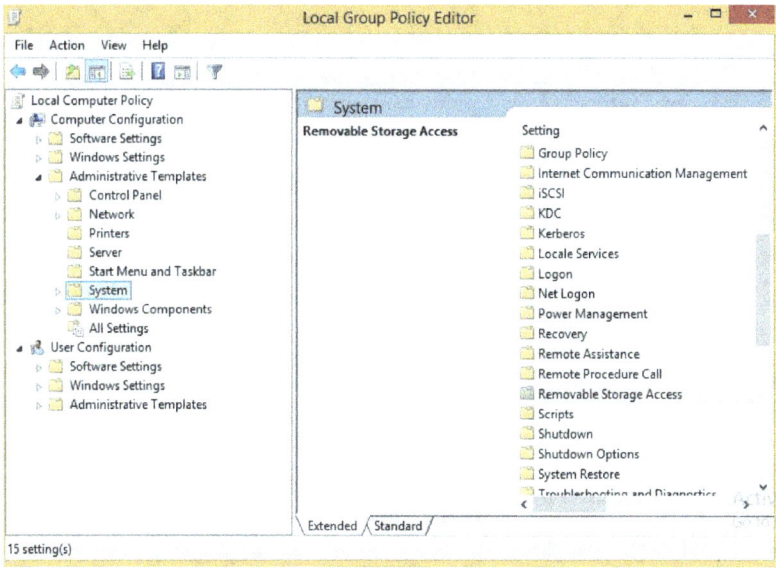

Figure 4.4 Local Policy

109

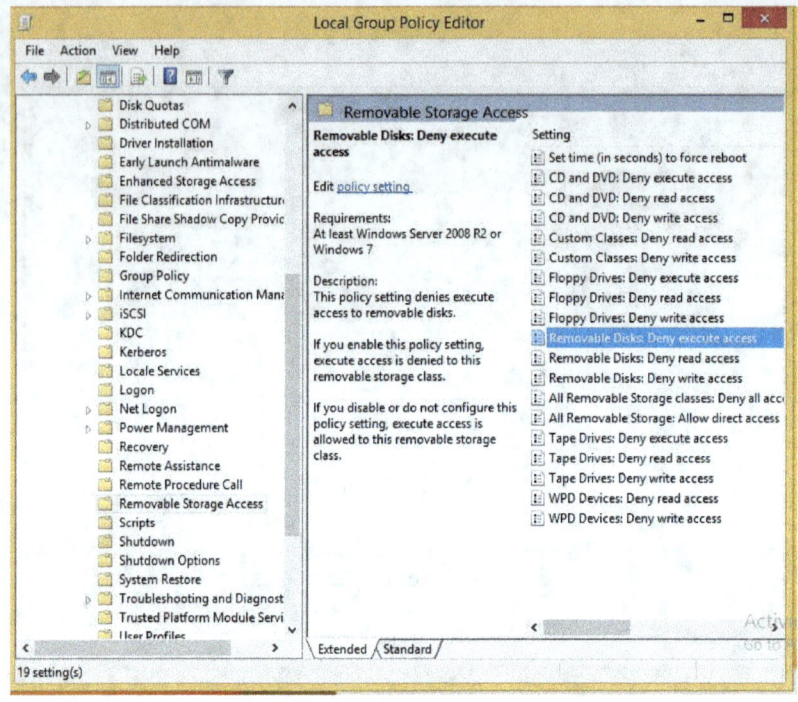

Figure 4.5 Removable storage access

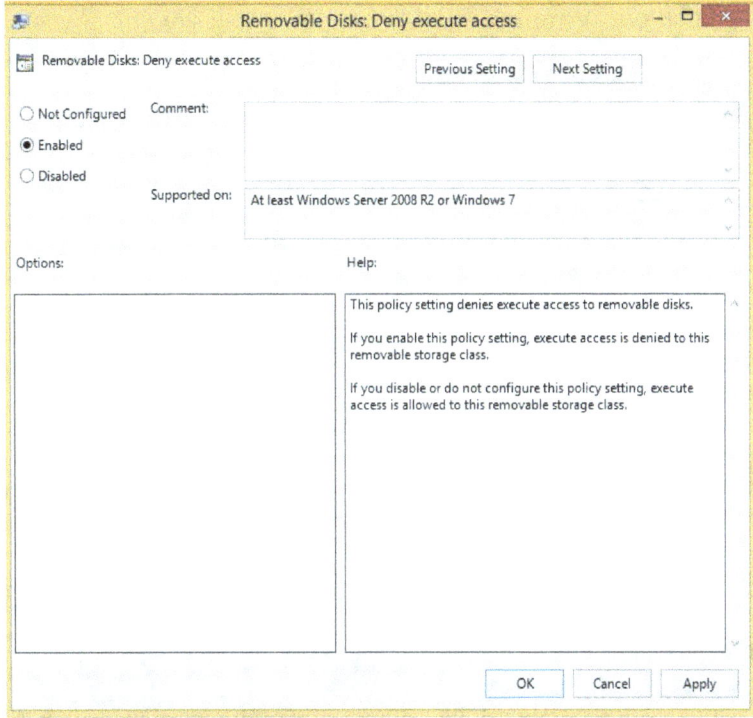

Figure 4.6 Removal Disks

3.23 INTERNET/NETWORKS

- Do not access sensitive information or use your credit card when connecting to a public hotspot.

- Ensure the website you want to use is secured before making online financial transactions. Check the webpage link.

- Use two/multi-factor authentication mechanisms.

- Block or filter the ping command.

- Update your browser. We recommend using Google Chrome.

- Disable the SSID of the router.

- Reduce the broadcast power of your Wi-Fi.

- Disable the WPS feature on the Network.

- Enable strong encryption on the router, and do not use WEP. We recommend using WPA2 or WPA3.

- Monitor and check the network traffic.

- Automatically connecting to networks can create vulnerabilities exploitable by hackers and others. Switch off your Wi-Fi and Bluetooth connections when not in use. Also, disable the auto connection to the Wi-Fi.

- Avoid clicking on any pop-up windows that claim your computer is infected with a virus. Turn off the active scripting option in the browser, so that scripts are not automatically executed on the browser (Paul, 2011).

3.24 SOCIAL MEDIA

- Limit your personal information on social media, such as Facebook, Instagram, etc.

- Restrict the availability of your profile only to your friends.

- Postpone publishing your pictures when you are on a trip until you return home.

- Disable the location feature on the camera and your pictures.

- Use multi-factor authentication mechanisms. Use a token to log in, as well.

- Remember to sign out when using public computers, like those in the library.

3.25 MOBILE SAFETY TIPS

1. Keep the amount of stored data and confidential information to a minimum.

2. During storage and transmission, always encrypt your sensitive data.

3. Be sure to thoroughly erase all data before disposing of or reusing the mobile device.

4. Activate a remote data wiping feature when available.

5. Keep your software up to date.

6. Utilize two-step authentication when available.

7. Always use the most up-to-date versions of your mobile operating system, security software, apps, and web browsers.

8. When on an unfamiliar network, be sure to enable two-step authentication (if it's available) and to change the password for any accessed account.

9. On a public or unsecured wireless connection, avoid websites and apps that require personal information, such as log-ins, whenever possible.

10. Be sure to turn off Wi-Fi and Bluetooth connections when they are not in use. Being connected to such networks exposes you to the risk of being hacked or exploited.

3.26 Holiday Traveling with Personal Internet-Enabled Devices

Avoid using public wireless networks.

Avoid using public networks when banking, doing business, and shopping online. Unsecured public Wi-Fi is an easy target for attackers to intercept your transactions and access unencrypted sensitive information.

Turn off Bluetooth when you are not using it.

Be sure to disable your Bluetooth setting when you are not using your device. Although Bluetooth is a very convenient feature, an open Bluetooth connection can be breached by cybercriminals, who can then access your sensitive data.

Be cautious when charging.

Charging your mobile device on a public charging station (like those you might find at an airport), or an unknown computer is risky. Such sources could contain malware and therefore could infect your mobile device. Avoid connecting to them if at all possible.

Avoid becoming a target of deceptive phishing schemes.

Shopping online poses security risks. Be careful to avoid phishing and other scams associated with online shopping. If you receive an email from a retailer that contains a link or an attachment or offers a deal that seems too good to be true, don't click it on; ignore it.

3.27 IMPORTANT RESOURCES

It's critical to be well-prepared and educated in cyberspace. Educated users will optimize their defenses against attackers. In this section you can find a list of recommended resources for the most recent threats, the most common attacks, and the best countermeasures. You can also find tips to keep you informed and up-to-date in the fight against cybercriminals.

- Cybersecurity Infrastructure Security Agency, https://www.cisa.gov/

- Federal Trade Commission Consumer Advice, https://consumer.ftc.gov/identity-theft-and-online-security

- Cybersecurity News and Blog, https://news.trendmicro.com/category/security/

- TrendMicro free tools, https://www.trendmicro.com/en_us/forHome/products/free-tools.html

- Free link reporting resource: https://www.ic3.gov/

- Common Vulnerabilities and Exposures, https://cve.mitre.org/

- Common Attack Pattern Enumeration and Classification, https://capec.mitre.org/

- Common Weakness Enumeration, https://cwe.mitre.org/

- Dr. Rafeeq's YouTube channel, https://www.youtube.com/watch?v=Lmf9yxwge5Y&list=PLtFOjtV0ZU8aWJlIaJvEOWs0ZdqRE-btb

About the author

Dr. Rafeeq Al-Hashemi is a professor at Illinois Central College. He is a Ph.D. holder in Computer Science. Al-Hashemi is Cisco Networking and Security+ certified. Dr. Al-Hashemi's passion is teaching and  researching. He has twenty years of experience in the classroom, instructing various computer science subjects, including Cyber Security, Artificial Intelligence, and Secure Software. He has been recognized as a Cybersecurity Champion by the NCSA. Dr. Al-Hashemi, an IEEE senior member, has published many well-received research papers in notable peer-reviewed journals.

7. REFERENCES

ALEXANDER, V., JOSE, M., & ANGELA , H. (2017, May 31). *Ransomware: Best Practices for Prevention and Response*. Retrieved from https://www.sei.cmu.edu/: https://insights.sei.cmu.edu/sei_blog/2017/05/ransomware-best-practices-for-prevention-and-response.html

America's Cyber Defense Agency. (2023). *Shopping Safely Online*. Retrieved from Cybersecurity infrastrucure security agency: https://www.cisa.gov/news-events/news/shopping-safely-online

Apple. (2023, April 26). *What to do before you sell, give away, or trade in your iPhone or iPad*. Retrieved from https://www.apple.com/: https://support.apple.com/en-us/HT201351

Belcic, I. (2020, May 14). *What is a Sniffer, and How Can I Protect Against Sniffing?* Retrieved from https://www.avast.com/: https://www.avast.com/c-sniffer

BIS. (2023). *Symtoms spyware infection*. Retrieved from www.askbis.com: https://www.askbis.com/9-symtoms-spyware-infection

Conklin, W. A. (2016). *Principles of Computer Security*. Mc Graw Hill Education.

Disotto, J.-A. (2023, March 1). *How to wipe all personal data and erase your iPhone and iPad*. Retrieved from https://www.imore.com/: https://www.imore.com/how-wipe-all-your-personal-data-ipad-or-iphone

Federal Trad Commission. (2023). *Warning Signs of Identity Theft*. Retrieved from https://www.identitytheft.gov/#/Warning-Signs-of-Identity-Theft

GEBHART, G. (2016, Dec 9). *How To Enable Two-Factor Authentication on Gmail and Google*. Retrieved from https://www.eff.org/: https://www.eff.org/deeplinks/2016/12/how-enable-two-factor-authentication-gmail-and-google

Identity theft. (2023, May 21). Retrieved from Wikipedia: https://en.wikipedia.org/wiki/Identity_theft

Kaspersky. (2023, May 2023). *What is a Trojan horse and what damage can it do?* Retrieved from Kaspersky: https://usa.kaspersky.com/resource-center/threats/trojans

Kaspersky. (2023). *What is Spyware?* Retrieved from https://usa.kaspersky.com/resource-center/threats/spyware

Microsoft Security Intelligence Report. (2017). *Microsoft Security Intelligence Report*. Microsoft.

Paul, M. (2011). *Guide to the CSSLP ((ISC)2*. CRC Press.

Protect Yourself Against Phishing Scams & Identity Theft. (2023, May 21). Retrieved from University of Massachusetts Amherst: https://www.umass.edu/it/support/security/protect-yourself-against-phishing-scams-identity-theft

Rafail, M. M. (n.d.). *Evaluating Your Web Browser's Security Settings*. Retrieved from https://www.us-cert.gov/ncas/tips/ST05-001

Savvides, L. (2017, Dec 4). *How to wipe your phone or tablet before you sell it*. Retrieved from https://www.cnet.com/: https://www.cnet.com/tech/mobile/how-to-wipe-your-phone-or-tablet-before-selling/

Securing Wireless Networks. (2023, May 21). Retrieved from https://www.cisa.gov/: https://www.us-cert.gov/ncas/tips/ST05-003

Security Tips for Using Mobile Applications. (2023, May 21). Retrieved from InfoSec: https://www.infosec.gov.hk/english/yourself/mobileApps.html

Singha, R. (2018, April 12). *8 TIPS TO AVOID A SPYWARE ATTACK*. Retrieved from https://blogs.quickheal.com/8-tips-to-avoid-a-spyware-attack

Technology University Information. (2018, 1 18). *ARCHIVED: What are stealth, polymorphic, and armored viruses?* Retrieved from https://kb.iu.edu/d/aehs

Tomar, P. (2014, July). Combating Cyber Crime. Delhi.

USA gov. (2023, April 17). *Identity theft*. Retrieved from USAgov: https://www.usa.gov/identity-theft

Wikipedia. (2023, May 24). *Identity theft*. Retrieved from https://en.wikipedia.org/wiki/Identity_theft

www.ingramcontent.com/pod-product-compliance
Lightning Source LLC
Chambersburg PA
CBHW071833210526
45479CB00001B/122